The Art of the
PUT-DOWN

The Art of the
PUT-DOWN

Winifred Coles

canary
press

ISBN: 978-1-907795-66-4

Canary Press
An imprint of Omnipress Ltd
Chantry House, 22 Upperton Road
Eastbourne, East Sussex BN21 1BF
England

Printed and bound in India

10 9 8 7 6 5 4 3 2 1

Editor: Jennifer Davies
Production Manager: Benita Estevez
Cover and internal design: Anthony Prudente

CONTENTS

INTRODUCTION

How often has an insult struck you dumb with anger, unable to think of the perfect riposte, only to come up with something later when your adversary has gone and any retort seems like sour grapes? The French have a term for it – *L'espirit de l'escalier* – meaning the moment at the bottom of the stairs when the rage-induced paralysis clears and you suddenly know exactly what you should have said. Alas, the moment has passed.

History is filled with characters who were never caught out at the wrong moment, or left gasping for words when an enemy made a smart, derogatory comment. Astonishingly adroit thinkers like Winston Churchill, Dorothy Parker, Oscar Wilde and Groucho Marx were never slow to seize the last word in any conversation. Churchill was especially skilful, able to cut his opponents down to size even in the white-hot arena of the British House of Commons. When Labour MP Bessie Braddock snapped, 'This is a disgrace. You are quite drunk', it was Churchill's off-the-cuff reply which became possibly the best put-down in history: 'And you, madam, are ugly. As for my condition, it will pass by the morning. You, however, will still be ugly.'

They just don't make insults like they used to, so plunder the past for great comebacks and watch your office nemesis wither with shame when you leave them lost for words.

CRUEL
BRITANNIA

Art & Architecture

His pictures seem to resemble not pictures but a sample book of patterns of linoleum.
Cyril Asquith, barrister, judge and son of Prime Minister Herbert Asquith, on the work of artist Paul Klee

....

The only major influence on Bacon has been his own surname.
Julian Barnes, writer, on artist Francis Bacon

....

Of course, we all know that Morris was a wonderful all-round man, but the act of walking round him always tired me.
Max Beerbohm, writer and caricaturist, on artist, writer and designer William Morris

....

I mock thee not, though I by thee am mocked; Thou call'st me madman, but I call thee blockhead.

William Blake, painter and poet, on sculptor John Flaxman

....

Why did you paint it so large? A small canvas might have concealed your faults.
William Hazlitt, writer and critic, on a painting by artist Benjamin Hayden

There are times when art aspires almost to the dignity of manual labour.
Oscar Wilde, writer and poet

....

I have been to it and am pleased to find it more odious than I ever dared hope.
Samuel Butler, novelist, on an exhibition of paintings by artist Dante Gabriel Rossetti

....

A monstrous carbuncle on the face of a much-loved and elegant friend.
Prince Charles on the proposed Sainsbury Wing extension to the National Gallery in London

Mr. Whistler always spelt art, and we believe he still spells it, with a capital 'I'.
Oscar Wilde on artist James McNeill Whistler

....

The world is rid of Lord Byron, but the deadly slime of his touch still remains.
John Constable, artist

....

She has the smile of a woman who has just dined off her husband.
Lawrence Durrell, novelist, on Leonardo da Vinci's painting *Mona Lisa*

....

It looks like a typewriter full of oyster shells; like a broken Pyrex casserole dish in a brown cardboard box.
Clive James, writer and critic, on Sydney Opera House

It makes me look like I'm straining a stool.

Winston Churchill on a portrait of himself by Graham Sutherland

Oscar Wilde, to James McNeill Whistler, on hearing him make a witty remark:
I wish I'd said that!
James McNeill Whistler:
You will, Oscar, you will!

....

James McNeill Whistler, to Oscar Wilde:
I went past your house this afternoon.
Oscar Wilde:
Thank you.

....

The only proof of taste Beckford has shown with his collection is getting rid of it.
William Hazlitt on the donation of the William Beckford art collection to a museum

....

If I met Picasso in the street I would kick him in the pants.
Alfred Munnings, painter and outspoken critic of Modernism in art

....

A buffalo in wolf's clothing.
Robert Ross, art historian, on artist and writer Percy Wyndham Lewis

....

I have seen and heard much of cockney impudence before now; but never expected to hear a coxcomb ask two hundred guineas for flinging a pot of paint in the public's face.
John Ruskin, art critic, on James McNeill Whistler's painting *The Falling Rocket*

Celebrities & the Media

Arianna Stassinopoulos is so boring you fall asleep halfway through her name.

Alan Bennett, playwright and author, on the author and newspaper columnist

....

Remember, tonight isn't all about comedy. Here's Ben Elton!

Frankie Boyle, comedian, on television show *Mock the Week*

....

[The television is] an invention that permits you to be entertained in your living room by people you wouldn't have in your home.

David Frost, television personality, comedian and journalist

....

My biggest regret in life is saving David Frost from drowning.

Peter Cook, comedian

....

Taking your clothes off, doing sexy dancing and marrying a rich footballer must be very gratifying, your mother must be so proud.

Lily Allen, singer, to Cheryl Cole, singer and television presenter

....

That guy would bottle your pee and sell it for a fiver.

Ringo Starr, musician, on novelist and politician Jeffrey Archer

A suicidal, silicone-breasted, bleached-blonde, 40-year-old mother of four, adulterous spawn of Hughie Green and a Bluebell Girl, with a dead boyfriend, an even deader career and a habit of being sick into her handbag at parties.
Julie Burchill, writer and newspaper columnist, on Paula Yates, ex-wife of Bob Geldof and partner of the late INXS singer Michael Hutchence

....

This deadly, winking, sniggering, snuggling, scent-impregnated, chromium-plated, luminous, quivering, giggling, fruit-flavoured, mincing, ice-covered heap of mother love…
William Connor, writing as newspaper columnist *Cassandra*, on entertainer Liberace in the *Daily Mirror*

....

She's as dim as a light bulb in a power cut.
Sharon Osbourne on Australian singer Dannii Minogue

....

The man who wears his hair back to front.
Comedian Frankie Howard on David Frost

....

Jeffrey Archer has issued a strenuous denial – as good as a signed confession really!
Des Lynam, television presenter

....

You make the Queen sound rough.
Paul Merton, comedian, to posh-speaking art critic Brian Sewell

....

Like Anne Robinson in a Korean restaurant. It's dog eat dog.
Graham Norton, comedian and television presenter

Like the Queen, only grander.

Alison Pearson, novelist and journalist, on charity campaigner and model Heather Mills

....

Heather Mills is a liar. I wouldn't be surprised if we found out she's actually got two legs.

Jonathan Ross, talk-show host

....

Poor old Kate Moss. Looks like she's reached the end of the line. Luckily she's got another seven chopped out already.

Jonathan Ross

....

If Cher has another facelift she'll be wearing a beard.

Jennifer Saunders, actor, writer and comedian

....

Not satire, but name-dropping. He writes like a man who wishes he were invited to more parties.

Writer, Paul Theroux, on writer and critic Clive James

....

I didn't realise she had facial hair, I couldn't get past the Gene Wilder wig.

Sharon Osbourne on Britain's Got Talent winner Susan Boyle

....

Most comedians aren't funny in real life. Take Jennifer – she's so boring if you meet her. Her natural state is flatlining.

Ruby Wax, comedian, on Jennifer Saunders

Is it true that you make your own yoghurt – you get a pint of milk and stare at it?
Ted Robbins, comedian and broadcaster, to journalist and television presenter Anne Robinson

....

Is there any beginning to your talents?
Clive Anderson, television presenter, to Jeffrey Archer

....

Simon Cowell, judging a group on *X Factor*:
Contestant:

I always thought you were such a wonderful man. But you're not. We're good. All we need is some direction.

Simon Cowell:

The direction is over there. Go towards the door...

....

Mr Letterman is rather difficult to work for (as a guest) because he expects you to be funny, and frequently, but not quite as funny as he is.
Quentin Crisp, writer and raconteur, on talk-show host David Letterman

They should give gossip columnist Joyce Haber open-heart surgery – and go in through her feet.
Julie Andrews, actor and singer

....

Vile, the worst of British values posing as the best.
Alastair Campbell, writer and former Labour Party political aide, on the *Daily Mail*

....

His big asset: a face that would look well upon a three-toed sloth.

Russell Davies, journalist and broadcaster, on actor Sylvester Stallone

....

She has a face that belongs to the sea and the wind, with large rocking-horse nostrils and teeth that you know bite an apple every day.
Cecil Beaton, photographer, on actor Katharine Hepburn

....

Many people would no more think of entering journalism than the sewage business – which at least does us some good.
Stephen Fry, actor, writer and comedian

....

Charlie Chaplin was a second-rate bicycle acrobat who should have kept his mouth shut.
Kingsley Amis, writer

If you cannot get a job as a pianist in a brothel, you become a royal reporter.
Max Hastings, journalist

....

A miniscule balding lump of cynical lard.
Piers Morgan on *Private Eye* editor Ian Hislop

....

Simon Cowell, judging on *X Factor*:
Contestant: Okay, so you hate me. Is there anything I can do to improve?
Cowell: Leave.

....

Her forehead looks like a flatscreen TV.
Sharon Osbourne on Australian actor Nicole Kidman

....

Simon Cowell, to a contestant on *X Factor*:
That performance was as relevant as a cat turning up for Crufts.

....

Journalism: an ability to meet the challenge of filling the space.

Rebecca West, author and journalist

....

His features resembled a fossilized wash-rag.
Alan Brien, journalist, on actor Steve McQueen

Who can forget Mel Gibson in *Hamlet*? Though many have tried.

Harry Andrews, actor

....

No. The 't' is silent, as in 'Harlow'.

Margot Asquith, socialite, author and wit, to actor Jean Harlow, who had enquired whether the 't' in Margot was pronounced

....

One wishes that Julie Andrews did not always give the impression that she had just left her horse in your hallway.

Michael Billington, critic

....

Genetic defect, serial bee-stings, or, whisper it softly, collagen, I know not, but, whatever the cause of Garner's pout, the overall effect is that her top lip now enters the room several seconds before the rest of her.

Matthew Bond, journalist, on actor Jennifer Garner

....

It was like kissing the Berlin Wall.

Helena Bonham-Carter, actor, on kissing Woody Allen in the film *Mighty Aphrodite*

....

Peter Sellers was his own worst enemy, although there was plenty of competition.

Roy Boulting, film producer and director

....

He's fine, if you like acting with two and a half tons of condemned veal.

Coral Browne, actor, on a leading man

....

There have always been mixed opinions about Charles Bronson. Some people hate him like poison and some people just hate him regular.

Jill Ireland, actor and ex-wife of Charles Bronson

....

He's a disappointed narcissist.

Simon Callow on fellow actor Charles Laughton

....

Tallulah is always skating on thin ice, and everyone wants to be there when it breaks.

Mrs. Patrick Campbell on actor Tallulah Bankhead

....

Simon Cowell, judging on *X Factor*:

You came in, you called yourself Champagne and you sounded like House Wine. I mean that sort of sums up the performance – Champagne, you're flat.

....

Jamie Lee Curtis has trouble learning her lines because English is not her first language. She doesn't, unfortunately, have a first language.

John Cleese, actor and comedian

They *are* only ten.
Lord Northcliffe, newspaper proprietor, reminding his staff of the mental age of the readers of his newspapers

....

He has a face like two profiles stuck together.
Mrs. Patrick Campbell on actor Basil Rathbone

....

Julie Andrews is like a nun with a switchblade.

Leslie Halliwell, film historian

....

Last month Catherine Zeta Jones raised a few eyebrows with her flirty behaviour with veteran actor Sean Connery, a man old enough to be her husband.
Martin Clunes, actor

....

Mary Pickford was the girl every young man wanted to have... as his sister.
Alistair Cooke, journalist and broadcaster

....

The only moving thing about Charlton Heston's performance was his wig.
Michael Coveney, critic

....

You can't direct a Laughton picture. The best you can hope for is to referee.
Alfred Hitchcock on Charles Laughton

If you weren't the best light comedian in the country, all you'd be fit for would be the selling of cars in Great Portland Street.
Noël Coward, playwright, composer, director, actor and singer, to actor Rex Harrison

....

Spielberg isn't a filmmaker, he's a confectioner.
Alex Cox on fellow film director Steven Spielberg

....

Joan Collins is to acting what her sister Jackie is to literature.
Journalist, *Daily Express*

....

In his bodybuilding days Arnold Schwarzenegger was known as the Austrian Oak. Then he started acting and he was known as …the Austrian Oak.
Jack Dee, comedian

....

Dear Ingrid. Speaks five languages and can't act in any of them.
John Gielgud, actor, on actor Ingrid Bergman

....

She chose to hide her bushel under Charles Laughton's great big light.
Hermione Gingold, actor, on Charles Laughton's actor wife, Elsa Lanchester

....

Her virtue was that she said what she thought, her vice that what she thought didn't amount to much.
Peter Ustinov, actor, writer and dramatist, on gossip columnist Hedda Hopper

There have been times when I've been ashamed to take the money, but then I think of some of the movies that have given Olivier cash for his old age, and I don't feel so bad.

Stewart Granger on fellow actor Lawrence Olivier

....

Hedda Hopper was a mental defective. She wore corrective hats.

Stewart Granger

....

Julia Roberts is very big-mouthed. Literally, physically, she has a very big mouth. When I was kissing her, I was aware of a faint echo.

Hugh Grant, actor

....

A man of many talents, all of them minor.

Leslie Halliwell on film director Blake Edwards

....

Michael Caine compares himself to Gene Hackman. This is foolish. Hackman is an intimidating and dangerous actor. Mr. Caine is about as dangerous as Laurel and Hardy, or indeed both, and as intimidating as Shirley Temple.

Richard Harris on fellow actor Michael Caine

....

Pierce Brosnan always reminds me of the models in men's knitwear magazines.

Paul Hoggart, television critic and newspaper columnist

I've read that Bogarde's cruel streak can be attributed to his fight for acceptance as an actor, as a homosexual man, and as a writer. And all the time I thought it was just because he's quite an unpleasant fellow.

Michael Hordern on fellow actor Dirk Bogarde

....

Arnold Schwarzenegger looks like a condom full of walnuts.

Clive James

....

Santa Clause III is the cinematic equivalent of tertiary syphilis.

Mark Kermode, film critic

....

After Arnold Schwarzenegger, Dolph Lundgren is a bit of a disappointment. At least Arnold looks like he comes supplied with batteries.

Adam Mars-Jones, novelist and critic

....

Which part is he playing now?

W. Somerset Maugham, playwright, novelist and short story writer, on Spencer Tracy during filming of *Dr. Jekyll and Mr. Hyde*

....

I remember my brother once saying, 'I'd like to marry Elizabeth Taylor,' and my father said, 'Don't worry, your time will come.'

Spike Milligan, comedian and writer

To the unwashed public, Joan Collins is a star. But to those who know her, she's a commodity who would sell her own bowel movement.

Anthony Newley, actor, singer and ex-husband of Joan Collins

....

You always knew precisely where you stood with him because he always let you down.

David Niven on actor, Errol Flynn

....

George Sanders had a face, even in his twenties, which looked as though he had rented it on a long lease and had lived in it for so long he didn't want to move out.

David Niven

....

She unfortunately can't be with us tonight. She's busy attending the birth of her next husband.

John Parrot, snooker player and commentator, on actor Joan Collins

....

Would you ever consider keeping your clothes on if the script demanded it?

Comedian Paul Kay, as Dennis Pennis, to actor Demi Moore

....

I find you a little wooden. How do you psyche yourself up? Do you go into a forest and look at some trees?

Comedian Paul Kay, as Dennis Pennis, to Hugh Grant

• • • • • • • • • • • • • • • • • • •

Katharine Hepburn has a cheekbone like a death's head allied to a manner as sinister and aggressive as crossbones.

• • • • • • • • • • • • • • • • • • •

James Agate, diarist and critic

Working with Glenda Jackson was like being run over by a Bedford truck.

Oliver Reed, actor

....

Raquel Welch is someone I can also live without. We've got some love scenes together and I am dreading them!

Oliver Reed

....

They'd have to pay me an awful lot of money to work with Jim again.

Kate Winslet, actor, on working with James Cameron in *Titanic*

....

Jean-Claude Van Damme exudes the character of a packet of Cup-A-Soup.

Jonathan Romney, journalist

....

Tom Cruise is to become a father. So, we'll soon hear the pitter-patter of tiny feet...as Tom rushes down to the shop to get nappies.

Jonathan Ross

....

Liz Hurley longs for the day when people stop pointing cameras at her. Speaking as someone who has seen all her films, I couldn't agree more.

Jonathan Ross

The four-foot Pole you wouldn't want to touch with a ten-foot pole.
Kenneth Tynan, critic, on film director Roman Polanski

....

Anyone might become homosexual after seeing Glenda Jackson naked.
Auberon Waugh, novelist, after seeing her in the film *Women In Love*

....

Glenn Close is not an actress – she's an address.

Maggie Smith, actor

....

Peter O'Toole had a face not so much lived in, as infested.
Paul Taylor, journalist

....

To say she acts would be to over-stretch the truth.
Christopher Tookey, film critic, on actor and model Kelly Brook

....

He both looked and sounded like a cement mixer.
Kenneth Tynan on actor and comedian W. C. Fields

....

The vengeful hag is played by Ingrid Bergman, which is like casting Eleanor Roosevelt as Lizzie Borden.
Kenneth Tynan

....

Ah, Victor, still struggling to keep your head below water?
Emlyn Williams, actor and dramatist, to actor Victor Spinetti

Guys like him and Caine talk about acting as if they knew what it was.

Actor, Nicol Williamson, on Sean Connery and Michael Caine

....

Clearly newsreader Natasha Kaplinsky is to become the acceptable face of BBC dumbing down. They certainly don't come much dumber.

Amanda Platell, journalist

....

Jennifer Saunders is a one-trick horse; Dawn French is a one-trick carthorse.

A. A. Gill, journalist and critic

....

He was once hired by the BBC to make Anne Robinson look funny but her plastic surgeon beat him to it.

Trevor McDonald, newsreader, *Have I Got News for You*

....

This is a general knowledge game, not a home for the bewildered.

Anne Robinson, journalist and quiz show host, to a contestant on quiz show, *The Weakest Link*

....

The amount of money he's earned for not making me laugh is staggering.

Will Self, novelist, on comedian Frank Skinner

What do ITV and fish fingers have in common? After two or three minutes, you have to turn them over.
Frank Skinner

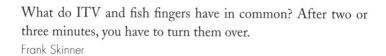

I once bumped into Sally Field by the pool in a big Hollywood hotel, and time, it must be said, had not been kind to the former screen goddess – in fact, it hadn't even been mildly understanding.
Dylan Jones, journalist

David Hasselhoff: more wooden than Pinocchio with a stiffie.

Mark Lamarr, comedian and television presenter

Boring and brain-crippling... Leona Lewis and Alexandra Burke are at the mercy of the next song they can get. It's important they write their own songs, so they're not at the mercy of anyone. Songwriters today are pretty awful, which is why everything sounds the same. Contemporary pop music isn't very inspiring.
Elton John on *X Factor* and contemporary pop music

The live feed of *Celebrity Big Brother* operates on a 15-minute delay, which caused confusion when Jimmy Saville entered the house as he operates on a 30-year delay.
Dara O'Briain, comedian

Literature

When you were quite a little boy somebody ought to have said 'hush' just once.

Patrick Campbell, actor, to playwright George Bernard Shaw

....

The way Bernard Shaw believes in himself is very refreshing in these atheistic days when so many people believe in no God at all.

Israel Zangwill, writer

....

Playwright George Bernard Shaw to Winston Churchill:

I am enclosing two tickets to the first night of my new play; bring a friend... if you have one.

Winston Churchill's response to George Bernard Shaw:

Cannot possibly attend first night; will attend second, if there is one.

....

There was little about melancholy that he didn't know; there was little else that he did.

W. H. Auden on fellow poet Alfred, Lord Tennyson

....

This is one of those big, fat paperbacks, intended to while away a monsoon or two, which, if thrown with a good over-arm action, will bring a water buffalo to its knees.

Nancy Banks-Smith, critic, reviewing M. M. Kaye's *The Far Pavilions*

The pompous preacher of melancholy moralities.
Jeremy Bentham, jurist, philosopher and social reformer, on writer and poet Samuel Johnson

....

Concerning no subject would he be deterred by the minor accident of total ignorance from preening a definitive opinion.
Roger Scruton, philosopher and writer on George Bernard Shaw

....

Gibbon is an ugly, affected, disgusting fellow and poisons our literary club for me. I class him among infidel wasps and venomous insects.
James Boswell, lawyer, diarist and author, on historian and politician Edward Gibbon

....

George Bernard Shaw: the spinster aunt of English literature.
Kenneth Tynan, critic

....

This enormous dunghill.
Writer and philosopher, Voltaire on playwright, William Shakespeare

....

One must have a heart of stone to read the death of little Nell without dissolving into tears... of laughter.
Writer and poet, Oscar Wilde, on novelist Charles Dickens' work *The Old Curiosity Shop*

....

You know I can't stand Shakespeare's plays, but yours are even worse.
Leo Tolstoy, Russian writer, to Russian playwright Anton Chekhov, after seeing his play, *Uncle Vanya*

The stupid person's idea of the clever person.
Elizabeth Bowen, on fellow novelist, Aldous Huxley

....

George too Shaw to be Good.
Dylan Thomas, poet

....

Frankly, I would prefer to read a novel about civil servants written by a rabbit.
Craig Brown, satirist, on the novel *Watership Down*, by former civil servant, Richard Adams

....

He festooned the dung heap on which he had placed himself with sonnets as people grow honeysuckle around outdoor privies.

Quentin Crisp, writer and raconteur on Ocsar Wilde

....

It was very good of God to let Thomas Carlyle and Mrs. Carlyle marry one another and so make only two people miserable instead of four.
Samuel Butler, novelist

....

He has said or done nothing worth a serious man taking the trouble of remembering.
Thomas Carlyle, writer, on poet Percy Bysshe Shelley

A tadpole of the lakes.
Lord Byron on fellow poet, John Keats

....

That insolent little ruffian. When he quitted a sofa, he left behind him a smear.
Norman Cameron on poet, Dylan Thomas

....

A hoary-headed and toothless baboon.

Thomas Carlyle, on Ralph Waldo Emerson

....

A dirty man with opium-glazed eyes and rat-taily hair.
Lady Frederick Cavendish, on poet Alfred, Lord Tennyson

....

Gibbon's style is detestable; but it is not the worst thing about him.
Samuel Taylor Coleridge, poet, on historian Edward Gibbon

....

It is clear then, nothing is wanting but the mind.
Charles Lamb, writer, on being told that poet William Wordsworth has said he felt more than up to the task of writing like Shakespeare, 'if he had a mind to try it.'

....

He would not blow his nose without moralizing on the conditions of the handkerchief industry.
Cyril Connolly on fellow writer George Orwell

What a tiresome, effected sod.

Actor and playwright, Noël Coward on Oscar Wilde

....

Life to Shaw is not a poem but a series of police regulations.

H. L. Mencken, writer on George Bernard Shaw

....

Oscar Wilde's talent seems to me to be essentially rootless, something growing in glass on a little water.

Irish novelist, George Moore

....

There never was an imposter so hateful, a blockhead so stupid, a crank so variously and offensively daft. He makes me tired.

Journalist and writer, Ambrose Bierce, on Oscar Wilde

....

Mr. Eliot is at times an excellent poet and has arrived at the supreme eminence among English critics largely through disguising himself as a corpse.

Poet and critic, Ezra Pound, on poet T. S. Eliot

....

She looked like Lady Chatterley above the waist and the gamekeeper below.

Cyril Connolly, on fellow writer Vita Sackville-West

....

Mr. Wordsworth, a stupid man, with a decided gift for portraying nature in vignettes, never ruined anyone's morals, unless, perhaps, he has driven some susceptible persons to crime in a very fury of boredom.

Ezra Pound on fellow poet William Wordsworth

He hasn't an enemy in the world, and none of his friends like him.
George Bernard Shaw on Oscar Wilde

The work of a queasy undergraduate squeezing his pimples.

Writer Virginia Woolf on James Joyce's *Ulysses*

An animated adenoid.
Norman Douglas on fellow writer Ford Madox Ford

George Bernard Shaw uses the English language like a truncheon.
Max Beerbohm, writer and caricaturist

I loathe you. You revolt me stewing in your consumption... you are a loathsome reptile – I hope you die.
D. H. Lawrence to writer Katherine Mansfield

Henry James had a mind so fine that no idea could violate it.
T. S. Eliot

A coxcomb who would have gone into hysterics if a tailor had laughed at him.
Ebenezer Elliott, poet and steel founder, on Lord Byron

Oh, really. What exactly is she reading?
Dame Edith Evans, actor, on hearing that novelist and biographer
Nancy Mitford had been lent a villa in order to 'finish her book'

....

Who is this Pope I hear so much about? I cannot discover what
is his merit. Why will my subjects not write in prose?
George II on poet Alexander Pope

....

This man, I thought, had been a lord among wits but I find he is
only a wit among lords.
Samuel Johnson on Lord Chesterfield

....

Lord Byron writes with the thoughts of a city clerk in metropoli-
tan clerical vernacular.
Ford Madox Ford

....

I am reading Henry James… and feel myself as one encased in a
block of amber.
Virginia Woolf on writer, Henry James

....

Shakespeare is a drunken savage with some imagination whose
plays please only in London and Canada.
Voltaire, writer and philosopher

....

Her mind is a very thin soil, laid an inch or two upon very barren
rock.
Virginia Woolf on Katherine Mansfield

Conrad spent a day finding the *mot juste* and then killed it.
Ford Madox Ford on fellow novelist, Joseph Conrad

....

There is no arguing with Johnson; for when his pistol misses fire, he knocks you down with the butt end of it.
Oliver Goldsmith, writer and poet, on playwright Ben Johnson

....

The sovereign of insufferables. He had nothing to say and he said it.
Ambrose Bierce on Oscar Wilde

....

There are two ways of disliking poetry; one way is to dislike it, the other is to read Pope.
Oscar Wilde on Alexander Pope

....

He's got hold of the red meat of the English language and turned it into hamburgers.
Richard Gordon on fellow novelist, Ernest Hemingway

....

That's Kingsley Amis, and there's no known cure.
Robert Graves, poet

....

He writes his plays for the ages – the ages between 5 and 12.
George Jean Nathan on George Bernard Shaw

....

His verse…is the beads without the string.
Gerard Manley Hopkins on fellow poet Robert Browning

Monsieur Zola is determined to show that if he has not genius he can at least be dull.

Oscar Wilde on author Emile Zola

....

Virginia Woolf's writing is no more than glamorous knitting. I believe she must have a pattern somewhere.

Dame Edith Sitwell

....

I have striven hard to open English eyes to the emptiness of Shakespeare's philosophy, to the superficiality and second-handedness of his morality, to his weakness and incoherence as a thinker, to his snobbery, his vulgar prejudices, his ignorance, his disqualifications of all sorts for the philosophic eminence claimed for him.

George Bernard Shaw

....

Nature, not content with denying him the ability to think, has endowed him with the ability to write.

A. E. Houseman, poet, on an unknown writer

....

A fungus of pendulous shape.

Alice James, diarist and sister of Henry James, on novelist George Eliot

....

As a work of art it has the same status as a long conversation between two not very bright drunks.

Clive James, writer and critic, on Judith Krantz's *Princess Daisy*

I doubt that the infant monster has any more to give.
Henry James, on fellow writer Rudyard Kipling

....

A freakish homunculus germinated outside lawful procreation.

Playwright, Henry Arthur Jones on George Bernard Shaw

....

He is limp and damp and milder than the breath of a cow.
Virginia Woolf on writer E. M. Forster

....

He was dull in a new way, and that made many people think him great.
Samuel Johnson on poet, Thomas Gray

....

But not I should imagine, that contempt which familiarity breeds.
Robert Lowe, politician, after a colleague remarked that he had the greatest contempt for Greek philosopher Aristotle

....

None ever wished it longer.
Samuel Johnson, on John Milton's epic work, *Paradise Lost*

....

We have met too late. You are too old for me to have any effect on you.
James Joyce, author, to poet W. B. Yeats

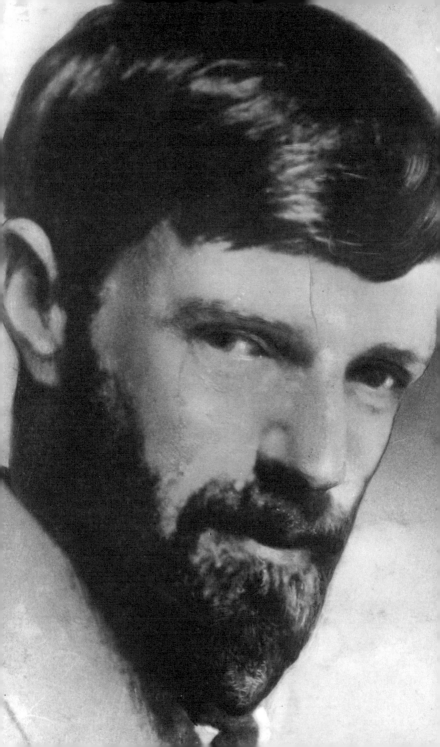

Mr. Lawrence looked like a plaster gnome on a stone barstool in some suburban garden... he looked as if he had just returned from spending an uncomfortable night in a very dark cave.

Dame Edith Sitwell, poet, on author D. H. Lawrence

The simplest clues to life escape him, as he scales impossible pinnacles of unnecessary thought, only to slip down the other side.

Edward Gordon Craig, actor, producer, director and theatre designer on George Bernard Shaw

....

Frank Harris is invited to all the great houses of England – once.

Oscar Wilde on author, editor and journalist, Frank Harris

....

Wordsworth has left a bad impression wherever he visited in town by his egotism, vanity and bigotry.

John Keats on fellow poet, William Wordsworth

....

He keeps one eye on a daffodil and the other on a canal share.

Walter Savage Landor, on fellow poet William Wordsworth

....

He grew up from manhood into boyhood.

R. A. Knox, theologian, priest and writer on writer G. K. Chesterton

....

For critics, I care the five-hundred-thousandth part of the tithe of a half-farthing.

Charles Lamb

....

The Sitwells belong to the history of publicity rather than of poetry.

F. R. Leavis, literary critic

Mad, bad and dangerous to know.
Lady Caroline Lamb, aristocrat and novelist, on Lord Byron

....

Sir, you have but two subjects, yourself and me. I am sick of both.
Samuel Johnson, to his biographer, James Boswell

....

An overgrown pimple, sore to the touch.

Quarterly Review, on writer and critic William Hazlitt

....

Nothing but old fags and cabbage-stumps of quotations from the Bible and the rest, stewed in the juice of deliberate, journalistic dirty-mindedness.
D. H. Lawrence, on the work-in-progress that would later become *Finnegan's Wake*, by James Joyce

....

The Hitler of the book racket.
Percy Wyndham Lewis, artist and writer, on novelist Arnold Bennett

....

The misfortune of Oliver Goldsmith in conversation is this: he goes on without knowing how to get off.
Samuel Johnson

....

The trouble with Ian Fleming is that he gets off with women because he can't get on with them.
Rosamond Lehmann, novelist

It is a better thing to be a starved apothecary than a starved poet. So go back to the shop, Mr. John. Back to plaster, pills and ointment boxes.
Jacob Gibson Lockhart, writer and editor, on poet John Keats

....

It was a book to kill time for those who liked it better dead.
Dame Rose Macaulay, writer

....

His imagination resembles the wings of an ostrich. It enabled him to run, though not to soar.
Thomas Babington Macaulay on poet John Dryden

....

The white and creamy look of an animated meringue.
Arthur Marshall, writer and broadcaster, on writer Barbara Cartland

....

Henry James had turned his back on one of the great events in the world's history, the rise of the United States, in order to report tittle-tattle at tea parties in English country houses.
W. Somerset Maugham, playwright, novelist and short story writer

....

I wish I was as sure of anything as Tom Macaulay is of everything.
Lord Melbourne, politician, on poet and historian, Thomas Babington Macaulay

....

To say Christie's characters are cardboard cut-outs is an insult to cardboard.
Ruth Rendell, novelist, on the work of crime writer Agatha Christie

....

Waldo is one of those people who would be enormously improved by death.

Saki, on fellow writer Ralph Waldo Emerson

....

In places, this book is a little over-written, because Mr. Blunden is no more able to resist a quotation than some people are to refuse a drink.

George Orwell, writer, on a book by poet Edmund Blunden

....

Freud Madox Fraud

Osbert Sitwell, poet, on Ford Madox Ford

....

George Eliot has the heart of Sappho; but the face, with the long proboscis, the protruding teeth of the Apocalyptic horse, betrayed animalist.

George Meredith, novelist and poet

....

A nice, acrid, savage, pathetic old chap.

I. A. Richards, literary critic, on American poet, Robert Frost

....

.. a sort of gutless Kipling.

George Orwell, on W. H. Auden

....

Oh, I see – one a year.

Denise Robins, to Barbara Cartland, after hearing she had written 145 books

He walked as if he had fouled his small clothes and looks as if he had smelt it.

Christopher Smart, poet, on Thomas Gray

....

He has occasional flashes of silence that make his conversation perfectly delightful.

Sydney Smith, writer and cleric, on writer Thomas Carlyle

....

A large shaggy dog unchained scouring the beaches of the world and baying at the moon.

Robert Louis Stevenson, novelist, on poet Walt Whitman

....

He has the most remarkable and seductive genius – and I should say about the smallest in the world.

Lytton Strachey, writer and critic, on Max Beerbohm

....

Reading him is like wading through glue.

Alfred, Lord Tennyson on playwright Ben Johnson

....

It is terribly hard not to dislike Evelyn Waugh.

Antonia White, writer

....

Isn't she a poisonous thing of a woman, lying, concealing, flipping, plagiarizing, misquoting, and being as clever a crooked literary publicist as ever.

Dylan Thomas, on fellow poet Dame Edith Sitwell

I never converse with a man who has written more than he has read.

Author Jonathan Swift, refusing to meet author Hugh Kelly

....

He has plenty of music in him, but he cannot get it out.

Alfred, Lord Tennyson on fellow poet Robert Browning

....

A louse in the locks of literature.

Alfred, Lord Tennyson on the critic Churton Collins

....

He's an old bore. Even the grave yawns for him.

Sir Herbert Beerbohm Tree, actor, on British-Jewish writer Israel Zangwill

....

If its length be not considered a merit, it hath no other.

Edmund Waller, poet, on John Milton's epic work, *Paradise Lost*

....

Like eating haggis, reading Dick Francis is something that must be done once but never again.

Guy Walters, author and journalist

....

To see him fumbling with our rich and delicate English is like seeing a Sevres vase in the hands of a chimpanzee.

Evelyn Waugh, novelist, on poet Stephen Spender

....

Do they keep throwing the book at Jeffrey Archer as an act of revenge for his lousy novels?

Keith Waterhouse, novelist and newspaper columnist

He is the old maid among novelists.
Rebecca West, author and journalist, on fellow author H. G. Wells

....

Fine words! I wonder where you stole them.
Jonathan Swift, to an unknown writer

....

As a bankrupt thief turns thief-taker, so an unsuccessful author turns critic.
Percy Bysse Shelley, poet

....

Your manuscript is both good and original; but the part that is good is not original, and the part that is original is not good.
Samuel Johnson to an unknown writer

....

Thomas Carlyle is a poet to whom nature has denied the faculty of verse.
Alfred, Lord Tennyson

....

He is every other inch a gentleman.
Rebecca West on novelist Michael Arlen

Music

Clive Anderson, television presenter, to the Bee Gees:

You're hit writers aren't you? I think that's the word anyway.

Barry Gibb:

That's the nice word.

Clive Anderson:

We're one letter short.

....

Beethoven's last quartets were written by a deaf man and should only be listened to by a deaf man.
Sir Thomas Beecham, conductor, on Ludwig van Beethoven

....

Sleeping with George Michael would be like having sex with a groundhog.
Boy George, singer

....

The musical equivalent of St. Pancras station.
Sir Thomas Beecham, on Edward Elgar's *Symphony in A Flat*

....

No, but I've stepped in it.
Sir Thomas Beecham, on being asked if he had ever played any Stockhausen

Have you seen U2's live show? It's boring as hell. It's like watching CNN.

Sharon Osbourne, television personality

....

Frankly, I'd rather listen to a pneumatic drill. She's nothing more than a spelling mistake – it should be Mary J. Bilge.

Jeremy Clarkson, journalist and broadcaster, on singer Mary J. Blige

....

No operatic tenor has yet died soon enough for me.

Sir Thomas Beecham

....

Composition, indeed! Decomposition is the word for such hateful fungi.

Critic on Franz Liszt in 1855

....

Luciano Pavarotti is only slightly smaller than Vermont.

Norman Lebrecht, critic and writer

....

Chris Martin looks like a geography teacher.

Liam Gallagher, musician, on Coldplay

....

Liam's only got two problems: everything he says and everything he does.

Noel Gallagher, musician, on his brother, Liam

....

Robbie Williams? You mean that fat dancer from Take That?

Noel Gallagher

A kind of musical Malcolm Sargent.
Sir Thomas Beecham, on the conductor Herbert von Karajan and
referring to his great rival Sir Malcolm Sargent

....

Armed with a wiggle and a Minnie Mouse squawk, she is coarse
and charmless.
Sheila Johnson, actor, on singer Madonna

....

The problem with Lloyd Webber's music is not that it sounds as
if it were written by other composers, but that it sounds as if it
were written by Lloyd Webber.
Gerald Kaufman, Labour politician, on the music of composer Andrew
Lloyd Webber

....

Peter Andre: the most unwelcome comeback since Jimi Hendrix's
vomit.
Mark Lamarr, television presenter

....

He sounds like he's got a brick dangling from his willy, and a
food mixer making puree of his tonsils.
Paul Lester, music journalist, on rock star Jon Bon Jovi

....

Billy Idol: the Perry Como of Punk.
John Lydon, singer

....

He plays four-and-a-half hour sets. That's torture. Does he hate
his audience?
John Lydon, on rock star Bruce Springsteen

He looks like a dwarf who's been dipped in a bucket of pubic hair.

Boy George, on fellow pop star Prince

There are some experiences in life which should not be demanded twice from any man, and one of them is listening to the *Brahms Requiem*.

George Bernard Shaw, playwright

....

No madam, he's decomposing.

W. S. Gilbert, composer, to a woman who asked him whether J. S. Bach was still composing

....

She is closer to organized prostitution than anything else.

Morrissey, singer, on Madonna

....

I had no idea Stravinsky disliked Debussy as much as this.

Sir Ernest Newman, music critic, on composer Igor Stravinsky's *Symphony of Wind Instruments* in memory of Claude Debussy

....

He sings like he's throwing up.

Andrew O'Connor, actor and comedian, on singer Bryan Ferry

....

To be Ozzy Osborne, it's not so bad. It could be worse, I could be Sting.

Ozzy Osborne, singer

....

I couldn't warm to him even if I was cremated next to him.

Keith Richards, musician, on rock and roll singer-songwriter Chuck Berry

His writing is limited to songs for dead blondes.
Keith Richards, on singer Elton John

....

Pink Floyd: the highlight of Live 8, if you count mustard gas as the highlight of World War I.
Mark Lamarr

....

Beethoven always sounded like the upsetting of bags – with here and there a dropped hammer.
John Ruskin, art critic

....

The chief objection to playing wind instruments is that it prolongs the life of the player.
George Bernard Shaw

....

She would be like Richard Wagner if only she looked a bit more feminine.
Osbert Sitwell, writer, on composer Dame Ethel Smyth

....

Wham split over the Gulf War – the gulf in talent between them.
Mark Lamarr

....

A provincial Debussy.
A. J. P. Taylor, historian, on composer Frederick Delius

Nationalities & Places

There are few more impressive sights in the world than a Scotsman on the make.

J. M. Barrie, Scottish author and dramatist

....

Oats: a grain which in England is generally given to a horse, but in Scotland it supports the people.

Samuel Johnson, writer and poet

....

A country to be in for two hours, to two and a half if the weather is fine, and no more. Ennui comes in the third hour, and suicide attacks you before the night.

Lord Brougham, statesman, on Switzerland

....

Thirty millions, mostly fools.

Thomas Carlyle, Scottish historian and essayist, when asked what the population of England was

....

They are a short, blue-vested people who carry their own onions when cycling abroad, and have a yard which is 3.37 inches longer than other peoples.

Alan Coren, writer and humorist, on the French

....

The Americans will always do the right thing... After they've exhausted all the alternatives.

Winston Churchill

Venice is excessively ugly in the rain – it looks like King's Cross.
Sir John Gielgud, actor

....

I am willing to love all mankind, except an American.

Samuel Johnson

....

The noblest prospect which a Scotchman ever sees, is the high road that leads him to England.
Samuel Johnson

....

Apart from cheese and tulips, the main product of Holland is advocaat, a drink made from lawyers.
Alan Coren

....

What a pity it is that we have no amusements in England but vice and religion.
Sydney Smith, writer and cleric

....

The purity of the air of Newfoundland is without doubt due to the fact that the people never open their windows.
J. G. Millais, artist and naturalist

....

Delhi is the capital of the losing streak. It is the metropolis of the crossed wire, the missed appointment, the puncture, the wrong number.
Jan Morris, writer

A kilt is an unrivalled garment for fornication and diarrhoea.

John Masters, novelist and soldier

Much may be made of a Scotchman, if he be caught young.

Samuel Johnson

....

The Irish are a fair people, they never speak well of one another.
Samuel Johnson

....

Americans have different ways of saying things. They say 'elevator', we say 'lift' ... they say 'President', we say 'stupid psychopath'
Alexei Sale, comedian and writer

....

A servile race in folly nursed.
Jonathan Swift, writer and cleric on the Irish

....

The Australian Book of Etiquette is a very slim volume.
Paul Theroux, writer

....

The land of my fathers, and my fathers can have it.
Dylan Thomas, poet, on Wales

....

There are still parts of Wales where the only concession to gaiety is a striped shroud.
Gwyn Thomas, poet

Politics

When I am right, I get angry. Churchill gets angry when he is wrong. We are angry at each other much of the time.
French General Charles de Gaulle on Prime Minister Winston Churchill

....

I wouldn't say she is open-minded on the Middle East so much as empty-headed. She probably thinks Sinai is the plural of Sinus.
Jonathan Aitken, politician, on Prime Minister Margaret Thatcher

....

He can't see a belt without hitting below it.
Margot Asquith, author, wit and wife of Prime Minister Herbert Asquith, on Prime Minister David Lloyd George

....

He knows nothing and thinks he knows everything. That points clearly to a political career.
George Bernard Shaw, playwright

....

Winston Churchill:
I venture to say that my Right Honourable friend, so redolent of other knowledge, knows nothing of farming. I'll even make a bet that she doesn't know how many toes a pig has.
Lady Astor, politician:
Oh, yes I do. Take off your little shoesies and have a look.

....

He has all the virtues I dislike and none of the vices I admire.
Winston Churchill on Labour politician Stafford Cripps

Sir Stafford Cripps has a brilliant mind until it is made up.
Attributed to both Margot Asquith and her stepdaughter, Lady Violet
Bonham Carter

....

I met Curzon in Downing Street, from whom I got the sort of greeting a corpse would give to an undertaker.
Prime Minister Stanley Baldwin, on statesman Lord Curzon

....

He is a mere cork, dancing in a current which he cannot control.
Prime Minister Arthur Balfour, on Prime Minister Henry Campbell-Bannerman

....

He brings to the fierce struggle of politics the tepid enthusiasm of a lazy summer afternoon at a cricket match.
Politician Aneurin Bevan, on Prime Minister Clement Attlee

....

Tony Blair is so weak and vulnerable now, Madonna is thinking of adopting him.
Rory Bremner, comedian and impressionist

....

He is a self-made man and worships his creator.

John Bright, politician, on Prime Minister Benjamin Disraeli

....

A crafty and lecherous old hypocrite whose very statue seems to gloat on the wenches as they walk the States House yard.
William Cobbett, journalist, on US Founding Father Benjamin Franklin

I have a fantasy where Ted Turner is elected President but refuses because he doesn't want to give up power.

Arthur C. Clarke, science fiction writer

....

Winston Churchill has devoted the best years of his life to preparing his impromptu speeches.

F. E. Smith, Conservative politician

....

Jeffrey Archer is proof of the proposition that within each of us lurks a bad novel.

Julian Critchley, politician

....

For the Blairs' official Christmas card Cherie decided not to smile, in case they couldn't fit the card into the envelope.

Ronnie Corbett, comedian, *Have I Got News for You*

....

Dear Randolph, utterly unspoilt by failure.

Noël Coward, playwright, composer, director, actor and singer on Winston Churchill's son Randolph

....

If a traveller were informed that such a man was the leader of the House of Commons, he might begin to comprehend how the Egyptians worshipped an insect.

Benjamin Disraeli on Lord John Russell, prime minister

....

He traces the steam train always back to the kettle.
Benjamin Disraeli, on Sir Robert Peel, prime minister and founder of the British police

．．．

His impact on history would be no more than the whiff of scent on a lady's handkerchief.
David Lloyd George, on Arthur Balfour

．．．

... he insults the House of Lords and plagues the most eminent of his colleagues with the crabbed malice of a maundering witch.
Benjamin Disraeli on the Earl of Aberdeen

．．．

Does the Honourable Lady remember that she was an egg herself once? And very many members of this House regret that it was ever fertilized.
Sir Nicholas Fairbairn, Conservative politician, to Junior Health Minister Edwina Currie, during the 1988 salmonella crisis

．．．

He would make a drum out of the skin of his mother in order to sound his own praises.
David Lloyd George on Winston Churchill

．．．

Like a cushion he always bore the impress of the last man who had sat on him.
Attributed to both David Lloyd George and Lord Haig, on Lord Derby

．．．

The great she-elephant.
Julian Critchley on Margaret Thatcher

She is a lady short on looks, absolutely deprived of any dress sense, has a figure like a Jurassic monster... very greedy when it comes to loot, no tact and wants to upstage everyone else.

Sir Nicholas Fairbairn, on Sarah Ferguson, Duchess of York

....

David Cameron plays by far the most convincing Blair. The rest of us just do the voice and mannerisms, but Cameron does the whole career.

Rory Bremner, on Prime Minister Tony Blair

....

Attila the Hen.

Clement Freud, broadcaster, writer and chef, on Margaret Thatcher

....

He only had one idea and that was wrong.

Benjamin Disraeli on a Member of Parliament

....

Mr. Attlee is a very modest man. But then he has much to be modest about.

Winston Churchill on Clement Atlee, prime minister

....

Neville has a retail mind in a wholesale business.

David Lloyd George on Prime Minister Neville Chamberlain

....

He is a man suffering from petrified adolescence.

Aneurin Bevan, politician, on Winston Churchill

....

Pétain in petticoats.

Denis Healey, on Margaret Thatcher

The right honourable and learned gentleman has twice crossed the floor of this House, each time leaving behind a trail of slime.
David Lloyd George on politician Sir John Simon

....

Being attacked in the House by him is like being savaged by a dead sheep.
Denis Healey, Labour politician, on Conservative politician Geoffrey Howe

....

I do not often attack the Labour party. They do it so well themselves.
Prime Minister Edward Heath

....

Mrs. Thatcher is doing for monetarism what the Boston Strangler did for door-to-door salesmen.
Denis Healey, on Margaret Thatcher

....

He has sat so long upon the fence that the iron has entered his soul.
David Lloyd George, on Sir John Simon

....

He has, more than any other man, the gift of compressing the largest amount of words into the smallest amount of thought.
Winston Churchill on Prime Minister Ramsay Macdonald

....

I thought he was a young man of promise; but it appears he is a young man of promises.
Arthur Balfour on Winston Churchill

The first man in twenty years to make the Presidency a part-time job, a means of filling up a few of the otherwise blank days of retirement.
Simon Hoggart, newspaper columnist, on President Ronald Reagan

It was said Mr. Gladstone could convince most people of most things, and himself of anything.
Dean William R. Inge, author and priest, on Prime Minister William Gladstone

She sounded like the Book of Revelations read out over a railway station public address system by a headmistress of a certain age wearing calico knickers.
Clive James, writer and critic, on Margaret Thatcher

La Pasionaria of middle-class privilege.
Denis Healey, on Margaret Thatcher

This goat-footed bard, this half-human visitor to our age from the hagridden magic and enchanted woods of Celtic antiquity.
John Maynard Keynes, economist, on David Lloyd George

He's a sheep in sheep's clothing.
Winston Churchill on Clement Atlee

The difference between a misfortune and a calamity is this: If Gladstone fell into the Thames, it would be a misfortune. But if someone dragged him out again, that would be a calamity.
Benjamin Disraeli

If Harold Wilson ever went to school without any boots, it was merely because he was too big for them.
Harold Macmillan, prime minister

....

George W. Bush studied the piano for several years before realizing it was a musical instrument made out of wood.
Paul Merton, comedian

....

The Right Honourable Gentleman's smile is like the silver fittings on a coffin.
Benjamin Disraeli, on Sir Robert Peel

....

She's democratic enough to talk down to anyone.

Austin Mitchell, Labour politician, on Margaret Thatcher

....

Dangerous as an enemy, untrustworthy as a friend, but fatal as a colleague.
Sir Hercules Robinson, colonial administrator, on politician, Joseph Chamberlain

....

Dull, Duller, Dulles.
Winston Churchill, on US Secretary of State John Foster Dulles

....

The Prime Minister has given the French President a piece of her mind, not a gift I would receive with alacrity.
Denis Healey, on Margaret Thatcher

He is not only a bore, but he bores for England.

Malcolm Muggeridge, writer and broadcaster, on Prime Minister Sir Anthony Eden

....

One could not even defy him with the name of a stuffed shirt. He was simply a hole in the air.

George Orwell, author and journalist, on Stanley Baldwin

....

Reminds me of nothing so much as a dead fish before it has had time to stiffen.

George Orwell on Clement Atlee

....

An empty taxi arrived at 10 Downing Street and when the door was opened, Atlee got out.

Winston Churchill on Clement Atlee

....

I must remind the Right Honourable Gentleman that a monologue is not a decision.

Clement Atlee to Winston Churchill

....

Tony Blair is the ultimate air guitarist of modern political rhetoric.

Will Self, writer

....

The right honourable gentleman is reminiscent of a poker. The only difference is that a poker gives off the occasional signs of warmth.

Benjamin Disraeli, on Sir Robert Peel

Jezebel.
Reverend Ian Paisley, Northern Irish politician, on Margaret Thatcher

....

Lord Beaverbrook's butler: His Lordship is out walking.
David Lloyd George: On the water, I presume.

....

Not a gentleman. Dresses too well.
Bertrand Russell, philosopher, on Prime Minister Anthony Eden

....

He might make an adequate Lord Mayor of Birmingham – in a lean year.
David Lloyd George, on Neville Chamberlain

....

They are not fit to manage a whelk stall.
Winston Churchill, on the Labour Party in 1945, the year he lost an election to it

....

I suspect English isn't his first language.
Linda Smith, comedian, on Labour politician John Prescott

....

In defeat unbeatable; in victory unbearable.
Winston Churchill on Viscount Montgomery

....

Michael Portillo seems to have his lips on inside out.
Linda Smith on the Conservative politician

....

Once a woman is made man's equal, she becomes his superior.
Margaret Thatcher

It is long, yet vigorous, like the penis of a donkey.
Sydney Smith, writer and cleric, on a work by statesman Henry Peter
Brougham

....

The Immaculate Misconception.

Norman St. John-Stevas, Conservative politician, on
Margaret Thatcher

....

The Right Honourable Gentleman is indebted to his memory
for his jests and to his imagination for his facts.
Richard Brinsley Sheridan, playwright and politician, on Henry Dundas,
politician

....

You don't reach Downing Street by pretending you've travelled
the road to Damascus when you haven't even left home.
Margaret Thatcher, on Labour leader Neil Kinnock

....

I've just learned about his illness; let's hope it's nothing trivial.
Winston Churchill on Labour politician Aneurin Bevan

....

He has not a single redeeming defect.
Benjamin Disraeli, on Prime Minister William Gladstone

....

Greater love hath no man than this, that he lay down his friends
for his life.
Jeremy Thorpe, Liberal leader, on hearing that Harold Macmillan had
fired half his cabinet in the 'Night of the Long Knives' in 1962

I do not see the EEC as a great love affair. It is more like nine middle-aged couples with failing marriages meeting at a Brussels hotel for a group grope.

Kenneth Tynan, critic

....

Lady Astor: **If you were my husband I'd poison your coffee.**
Winston Churchill: **If you were my wife, I'd drink it.**

....

I thought him fearfully ill-educated and quite tenth rate – pathetic. I felt quite maternal to him.

Hugh Walpole, novelist, on meeting Adolf Hitler

....

He has something of the night about him.

Anne Widdecombe, on fellow Conservative politician Michael Howard

....

A typical triumph of modern science to find the only part of Randolph that was not malignant and remove it!

Evelyn Waugh, novelist, on hearing that Winston Churchill's son, Randolph, had had a lung removed but it was found not to be cancerous

....

Harold Wilson is going round the country stirring up apathy.

William Whitelaw, Conservative politician

....

He has committed every crime that does not require courage.

Benjamin Disraeli on Irish lawyer, politician and agitator Daniel O'Connell

Earl of Sandwich:
I am convinced, Mr. Wilkes, that you will die either of the pox or on the gallows.
John Wilkes, politician, in reply:
That depends, Sir, on whether I embrace your mistress or your principles.

....

A shiver looking for a spine to run up.

Harold Wilson, Prime Minister, on Edward Heath

....

He immatures with age.
Harold Wilson, on Labour Party colleague Tony Benn

....

It is a reminder that *Morning Cloud's* skipper is no stranger to platitude and longitude.
Christopher Wordsworth, critic, reviewing Edward Heath's sailing-based book, *Travels* in the *Observer*.

....

Treachery with a smile on its face.
Margaret Thatcher, on being removed from office

Labour MP Bessie Braddock to Winston Churchill:

This is a disgrace. You are quite drunk.

Winston Churchill:

And you, madam, are ugly. As for my condition, it will pass by the morning. You, however, will still be ugly.

Royals

His intellect is no more use than a pistol packed in the bottom of a trunk if one were attacked in the robber-infested Apennines.
Prince Albert, on his son, Bertie, later King Edward VII

....

Now at least I know where he is.
Queen Alexandra, following the death of her womanizing husband, King Edward VII

....

Nowadays a parlour maid as ignorant as Queen Victoria was when she came to the throne would be classed as mentally defective.
George Bernard Shaw, playwright

....

Queen Anne was one of the smallest people ever set in a great place.
Walter Bagehot, constitutional historian, on Queen Anne

....

Very sorry can't come. Lie follows by post.
Baron Beresford, replying by telegram to a dinner invitation from Edward, Prince of Wales, the future King Edward VIII

....

No danger. For no man in England would take away my life to make you king.
King Charles II, to his brother, the Duke of York who had warned the king about travelling without guards

Who's your fat friend?
George 'Beau' Brummell, Regency dandy, to Beau Nash, who was
accompanied by the Prince Regent, the future King George IV

....

I cannot find it in me to fear a man who took ten years a-learning
of his alphabet.
Queen Elizabeth I, on King Philip II of Spain

....

What is there in the delivering over of a turgid blockhead and
an unprincipled prostitute into the hands of the hangman that it
should arrest for a moment attention.
Robert Burns, poet, on the execution of Louis XVI, and Marie Antoinette

....

Strip your Louis Quatorze of his king gear, and there is left nothing but a poor forked radish with a head fantastically carved.
Thomas Carlyle, writer, on King Louis XIV

....

Such an attractive lass. So outdoorsy. She loves nature in spite of what it did to her.

American singer and actor, Bette Midler, on Princess Anne

....

Buckingham Palace says the security system works. Presumably
much in the same way as Prince Charles works.
Angus Deayton, actor and television presenter, after a protester dressed
as Batman scaled a Buckingham Palace balcony

Camilla is so ugly she has to frisk herself at airports.
American actor Joan Rivers on Camilla Parker-Bowles

....

The plain truth is, that he was a most intolerable ruffian, a disgrace to human nature, and a blot of blood and grease upon the History of England.
Charles Dickens, writer, on King Henry VIII

....

...a pig, an ass, a dunghill, the spawn of an adder, a basilisk, a lying buffoon, a mad fool with a frothy mouth.
Martin Luther, German theologian and religious reformer, on King Henry VIII

....

King William blew his nose twice and wiped the royal perspiration from a face which is probably the largest uncivilized spot in England.
American writer Oliver Wendell Holmes, on King William IV

....

You have sent me a Flanders mare.
King Henry VIII, on prospective wife Anne of Cleves

....

The bloom of her ugliness is going off.
Sir Edward Cromwell Disbrowe, politician and diplomat, on the ageing Queen Charlotte, wife of King George III

....

I am unwell. Bring me a glass of brandy.
George, Prince of Wales, in 1795, on having kissed his bride-to-be, Princess Caroline of Brunswick, for the first time

I don't know his name but he's got a face like half a teapot.
King George VI, on actor Ralph Richardson

....

The wisest fool in Christendom.
King Henri IV, first Bourbon King of France, on James I of England

....

George the First was always reckoned
Vile, but viler George the Second;
And what mortal ever heard
Any good from George the Third?
When from Earth the Fourth descended
(God be praised!) the Georges ended.
Walter Savage Landor, writer and poet, on the four King Georges of
England

....

I found it ironic to hear the Queen reading her speech about
abolishing fox hunting wearing a dead stoat around her neck.
But that's not a nice way to talk about the Duke of Edinburgh.
Paul Merton, comedian

....

She looked like a huge ball of fur on two well-developed legs.

Nancy Mitford, novelist and biographer, on Princess
Margaret

....

In private life he would have been called an honest blockhead.
Lady Mary Wortley Montagu, writer, on King George I

She was happy as the dey was long.
Chief Justice Lord Norbury on Queen Caroline's affair with the Muslim Dey of Algiers

. . . .

If it doesn't eat hay, she is not interested.
Prince Philip, talking about horse-obsessed daughter, Anne, Princess Royal

. . . .

Fergie has been named Mother of the Year in the US. Who said the Yanks don't do irony.
Amanda Platell, journalist, on the Duchess of York

. . . .

The idea of Prince Charles conversing with vegetables is not quite so amusing when you remember that he's had plenty of practice chatting to members of his own family.
Jaci Stephen, journalist

. . . .

We don't come to Canada for our health. We can think of other ways of enjoying ourselves.

Prince Philip

. . . .

I married the Duke for better or worse, but not for lunch.
Wallis Simpson, Duchess of Windsor, after someone enquired why she and the Duke never lunched together

Mr. Gladstone speaks to me as if I were a public meeting.
Queen Victoria on William Gladstone

....

I thought men like that shot themselves.
King George V, on the 7th Earl Beauchamp who was having a
homosexual relationship

....

The Billy Carter of the British monarchy.
Robert Lacey, historian and biographer, on Princess Margaret

....

The thing that impressed me most about America is the way the
parents obey their children.
King Edward VIII

Sport

Devon Loch was a better finisher.

Ron Atkinson, football manager and pundit, on Aston Villa

....

Top hats look 100 per cent ridiculous on anybody, but on, for example, Willie Carson, it's like attaching a factory chimney to a bungalow.

Giles Smith, journalist, on the jockey and racing pundit

....

He cannot kick with his left foot, he cannot head a ball, he cannot tackle and he doesn't score many goals. Apart from that he's all right.

Footballer George Best, on footballer David Beckham

....

Football hooligans? Well, there are 92 club chairmen for a start.

Brian Clough, football manager

....

For years I thought the club's name was Partick Thistle Nil.

Billy Connolly, comedian

....

If David Seaman's dad had worn a condom, we'd still be in the World Cup.

Presenter of sports quiz *They Think It's All Over* Nick Hancock, on England goalkeeper, David Seaman

Ally McLeod thinks tactics are a new kind of mint.
Billy Connolly on the unsuccessful Scotland manager

....

Tony Hately had it all. The only thing he lacked was ability.
Tommy Docherty, football manager

....

I asked the Scottish Football Association if San Marino was a republic or a principality. They said it was a technicality.
Roddy Forsythe, football commentator

....

Brian Clough's record speaks for itself... if it can get a word in.
Cris Freddi, writer

....

I would like to thank the press from the heart of my bottom.

Nick Faldo, golfer

....

The only time Nick Faldo opens his mouth is to change his feet.
David Feherty, golfer

....

He has a face like a warthog that has been stung by a wasp.
David Feherty, on golfer Colin Montgomerie

....

What you've got to remember about Michael is that under that cold professional Germanic exterior beats a heart of stone.
Damon Hill, motor racing driver, on Michael Schumacher

He was as charming as always, which means that he was as charming as a dead mouse in a loaf of bread.
Clive James, writer and critic, on John McEnroe, tennis player

....

A cricketer – a creature very nearly as stupid as a dog.
Bernard Levin, journalist

....

You never know what's going on in his head, and often he doesn't seem to know himself.
Nigel Mansell, motor racing driver, on Nelson Piquet

....

Pass a ball? He'd have trouble passing wind.
Alf Ramsey, football manager, on Dutch international Piet Fransen

....

Kevin Keegan is not fit to lace George Best's drinks.

John Roberts, footballer

....

I know why he's bought a house by the sea – so that he'll be able to go for a walk on the water.
Fred Trueman, cricket commentator, on fellow cricketer Geoffrey Boycott

....

In one year I travelled 450,000 miles by air. That's 18 and a half times around the world, or once around Howard Cosell's head.
Jackie Stewart, motor racing driver, on the legendary US sports commentator

If Stan Bowles could pass a betting shop like he could pass a ball he'd have no worries at all.

Ernie Tagg, football manager

....

I remember when Steve Davis used to take valium as a stimulant.

Dennis Taylor, snooker player

....

He's like a human form of beige.

Linda Smith, comedian, on tennis player Tim Henman

Theatre

The sort of show that gives pornography a bad name.
Clive Barnes, critic, on *Oh, Calcutta!*

....

When you've seen all of Ionesco's plays, I felt at the end, you've seen one of them.
Critic Kenneth Tynan, on the work of Eugene Ionesco

....

The first man to have cut a swathe through the theatre and left it strewn with virgins.
Frank Harris, author and journalist, on playwright George Bernard Shaw

....

For those who missed it the first time, this is your golden opportunity: you can miss it again.

Michael Billington, critic, on a revival of the musical *Godspell* in 1981

....

Two things should be cut: the second act and the child's throat.
Noël Coward, playwright, composer, director, actor and singer

....

My Dear Sir, I have read your play. Oh, my dear Sir. Yours Faithfully.
Sir Herbert Beerbohm Tree, to a would-be dramatist

The best thing about Ian McKellen's *Hamlet* was his curtain call.

Harold Hobson, critic and author

....

Not content to have the audience in the palm of his hand, he goes one further and clinches his fist.

Kenneth Tynan, on an unknown actor

....

It should have been called *A Month in the Wrong Country*

Noël Coward, on the American adaptation of Anton Chekhov's *The Cherry Orchard*

Miscellaneous British Insults

Never in the history of fashion has so little material been raised so high to reveal so much that needs to be covered so badly.
Cecil Beaton, fashion designer, on the mini-skirt

....

Most women are not so young as they are painted.
Max Beerbohm, writer and caricaturist

....

If at first you don't succeed, failure may be your style.
Quentin Crisp, writer and raconteur

....

Journalist Sandra Harris, to novelist Barbara Cartland:
Have English class barriers broken down?
Barbara Cartland:
Of course they have, otherwise I wouldn't be sitting here talking to someone like you.

....

Twenty million young women rose to their feet with the cry 'We will not be dictated to!' and promptly became secretaries.
G. K. Chesterton, writer

....

I find it rather easy to portray a businessman. Being bland, rather cruel and incompetent comes naturally to me.
John Cleese, comedian and actor

We invite people like that to tea, but we don't marry them.
Lady Chetwode, on her future son-in-law, John Betjeman

....

Brigands demand your money or your life. Women demand both.
Samuel Butler, novelist

....

It's no accident that the symbol of a bishop is a crook, and the sign of an archbishop is the double-cross.
Dom Gregory Dix, English monk and liturgical scholar

....

Verily, it is easier for a camel to pass through the eye of a needle than for a scientific man to pass through a door.
Sir Arthur Eddington, Bristish scientist

....

A critic is a man created to praise greater men than himself, but he is never able to find them.
Richard Le Gallienne, author

....

Annoyed man in club to composer W. S. Gilbert:
I've just been grossly insulted. I overheard one of that crowd saying that he would offer me £50 to resign my membership.
W. S. Gilbert:
That's outrageous. You stick firm at a hundred and you'll get it.

....

He is not only dull himself; he is the cause of dullness in others.
Samuel Johnson, writer and poet

Diner, holding up a piece of food on the end of his fork and waving it about in front of the other diners:

Is this pig?

Douglas Jerrold, playwright:

To which end of the fork do you refer?

....

I won't eat anything that has intelligent life, but I'd gladly eat a network executive or a politician.

Marty Feldman, comedian and actor

....

She's the sort of woman who lives for others – you can tell the others by their hunted expression.

C. S. Lewis, novelist

....

Hostess, to Leonard Rossiter as he was leaving a party:

Do you have to leave so early?

Leonard Rossiter, actor and comedian:

No, it's purely a matter of choice.

....

A man may as well open an oyster without a knife, as a lawyer's mouth without a fee.

Barton Holyday, clergyman, author and poet

....

Come again when you can't stay so long.

Walter Sickert, English painter, saying goodbye to writer and painter, Denton Welch

....

Some folks are wise and some are otherwise.

Tobias George Smollett, poet and author

I am debarred from putting her in her place – she hasn't got one.

Dame Edith Sitwell, poet and critic, on an unknown woman

....

I regard you with an indifference bordering on aversion.

Robert Louis Stevenson, novelist and poet

....

She wears her clothes as if they had been thrown on by a pitchfork.

Jonathan Swift, satirist, poet and cleric

....

Critics search for ages for the wrong word, which, to give them credit, they eventually find.

Peter Ustinov, actor, writer and dramatist

....

British education is probably the best in the world, if you can survive it. If you can't there is nothing left for you but the diplomatic corps.

Peter Ustinov

....

Confession on Saturday. Absolution on Sunday. At it again on Monday.

H. G. Wells, writer, on Catholics

SCORN IN
THE USA

Art & Architecture

Abstract art? A product of the untalented, sold by the unprincipled, to the utterly bewildered.

Al Capp, cartoonist and humorist

....

Architect: one who drafts a plan of your house, and plans a draft of your money.

Ambrose Bierce, journalist and writer

....

Architecture is the art of how to waste space.

Philip Johnson, architect

....

A decorator tainted with insanity.

Kenyon Cox, critic, in *Harper's Weekly*, on Paul Gauguin, French painter

....

Friend to James McNeill Whistler:
There are only two great painters, you and Velasquez.
James McNeill Whistler:
Why drag in Velasquez?

....

A portrait is a painting with something wrong with the mouth.

John Singer Sargent, portrait painter

I can truthfully say that the painter has observed the Ten Commandments. Because he hath not made to himself the likeness of anything in heaven above, or that which is on earth beneath, or that which is in the water under the earth.
Abraham Lincoln, 16th president

....

If you were half a man... and you are.

Franklin P. Adams, newspaper columnist, to the vertically challenged artist and illustrator Reginald Birch

....

Frederick Leighton, to fellow artist James McNeill Whistler:
My dear Whistler, you leave your pictures in such a sketchy, unfinished state. Why don't you ever finish them?
James McNeill Whistler:
My dear Leighton, why do you ever begin yours?

....

The only genius with an IQ of 60.
Gore Vidal, author, playwright, essayist and political activist, on artist Andy Warhol

Celebrities & the Media

Why are we honoring this man? Have we run out of human beings?

Milton Berle, comedian, on sports commentator Howard Cosell

....

This is one Hilton that should be closed for renovation.

Richard Blackwell, known as 'Mr. Blackwell', fashion critic, on Paris Hilton

....

A woman whose face looked as if it had been made of sugar and someone had licked it.

George Bernard Shaw on American dancer Isadora Duncan

....

A senescent bimbo with a lust for home furnishings.

Barbara Ehrenreich, feminist, on Nancy Reagan

....

Is Elizabeth Taylor fat? Her favourite food is seconds.

Actor Joan Rivers

....

I've seen Don entertain 50 times and I've always enjoyed his joke.

Johnny Carson, talk-show host, on comedian Don Rickles

....

Marion Davies has two expressions: joy and indigestion.

Poet and wit Dorothy Parker

The only way Hugh Hefner can get stiff now is through rigor mortis.

Gilbert Gottfried, actor and comedian

....

Try interviewing her sometime. It's like talking to a window.

Bryant Gumbel, sports commentator, on Jerry Hall

....

I saw Angelina Jolie on TV. Those lips are so big, she could whisper in her own ear.

Joan Rivers

....

If you said 'irony' to Clay, he'd look down at his shirt and think it needed pressing.

Denis Leary, comedian, on fellow comedian Andrew Dice Clay

....

This Paula Jones woman is incredible. She says yes to posing nude in *Playboy*. She says yes to boxing Tonya Harding. The only thing too sleazy for her is Bill Clinton.

Jay Leno, talk-show host

....

Milton Berle is an inspiration to every young person that wants to get into show business. Hard work, perseverance, and discipline: all the things you need when you have no talent.

Dean Martin, actor, comedian and singer

....

Why are O. J. Simpson and Heidi Fleiss such bad golfers? Because he's a slicer and she's a hooker.

Robert Mitchum, actor

Joan Crawford has slept with every male star at MGM except Lassie.

Bette Davis

Gossip columnist Rona Barrett doesn't need a steak knife. She cuts her food with her tongue.

Johnny Carson

....

The reason I drink is because when I'm sober I think I'm Eddie Fisher.

Dean Martin

....

Rush Limbaugh is back at work. Doctors said his rehab was successful, but it could be weeks before he's a hundred percent self-righteous.

Jay Leno

....

Paris Hilton is doing a reality show, *I'm a Celebrity, Get Him Out of Me*.

Joan Rivers

....

Pamela Lee said her name is tattooed on her husband's penis which explains why she's changed her name from Anderson to Lee.

Conan O'Brien, talk-show host, on rock star and husband of Pamela Anderson, Tommy Lee

....

Jane Fonda and Ted Turner broke up. Jane found God and Ted found it wasn't him.

Robin Williams, comedian

The four pillars of wisdom that support journalistic endeavours are: lies, stupidity, money-grubbing and ethical irresponsibility.
Marlon Brando, actor, on the press

....

An enchanting toad of a man.
Helen Hayes, actor, on newspaper columnist Robert Benchley

....

We don't airbrush to that extent.
Hugh Hefner, on media personality Kelly Osborne's hopes of becoming a pin-up in his magazine *Playboy*

....

The DVD of Mariah Carey's movie *Glitter* is coming out with bonus features. Maybe one of them will be a plot.
Joan Rivers

....

She looks like something that would eat its young.
Dorothy Parker on actor Dame Edith Evans

....

I love the media. They should all be working from Dachau.
Jerry Lewis, comedian

....

Every journalist has a novel in him, which is an excellent place for it.
Russell Lynes, writer and art historian

....

I wish I could sue the *New York Post* but it's awfully hard to sue a garbage can.
Paul Newman, actor

Boy George is all England needs – another queen who can't dress.

Joan Rivers

....

Paris Hilton said she turned down plans for a life-size Paris Hilton doll even though they would have sold for $50,000 each. Paris questioned why you would pay $50,000 for a look-alike if you could have the real thing for three drinks.

Conan O'Brien

....

She must use novocaine lipstick.

Jack Parr, talk-show host, on journalist Dorothy Kilgallen

....

Murdoch's *Sun* has the class of a polyester shirt and the soul of a Colombian hit-man.

Washington Post on the British tabloid

....

Several tons of dynamite are set off in this John Wayne picture – none of it under the right people.

James Agee, author and critic

....

An associate producer is the only guy in Hollywood who will associate with the producer.

Fred Allen, comedian

....

Her acidic bons mots were the olives of the martini age.

Vanity Fair, on Dorothy Parker

Elizabeth Taylor has more chins than the Chinese telephone directory.
Joan Rivers

....

When Jack Benny plays the violin, it sounds as if the strings are still back in the cat.
Fred Allen

....

Her hair lounges on her shoulders like an anaesthetized cocker spaniel.
Journalist and critic Henry Allen, on actor Lauren Bacall

....

Drew Barrymore sings so badly, deaf people refuse to watch her lips move.
Woody Allen, comedian and film director

....

Scumbag.
Ed Asner, on fellow actor Charlton Heston

....

When Al Jolson attends a wedding he wants to be the bride and when he attends a funeral, he wants to be the corpse.
Lou Anthony, composer

....

All Angelina Jolie wants to do is do good for people. And she was saying to me, 'If I could just make one person happy, Joan, I'll die satisfied.' I said, 'Easy! Just give Jennifer Aniston back her husband.'
Joan Rivers

With Mick Jagger's lips, he could French-kiss a moose.
Joan Rivers

....

When I get hold of her, I'll tear every hair out of her moustache!
Tallulah Bankhead, on fellow actor Bette Davis

....

Katharine Hepburn isn't really stand-offish. She ignores everyone equally.
Lucille Ball, comedian

....

If I found her floating in my pool, I'd punish my dog.
Joan Rivers on Yoko Ono

....

Bette Davis and I are good friends. There's nothing I wouldn't say to her face – both of them.
Tallulah Bankhead

....

That's the kind of face you hang on your door in Africa.
Joan Rivers on fashion designer Donatella Versace

....

She has breasts of granite and a mind like Gruyere cheese.
Billy Wilder on Marilyn Monroe

....

A woman went to a plastic surgeon and asked him to make her look like Bo Derek. He gave her a lobotomy.
Joan Rivers

She is so hairy, when she lifted up her arm, I thought it was Tina Turner in her armpit.
Joan Rivers on Madonna

....

There's less to this than meets the eye.
Tallulah Bankhead, on a Broadway flop

....

I knew Elizabeth Taylor when she didn't know where her next husband was coming from.

Anne Baxter, actor

....

I have a previous engagement which I will make as soon as possible.
Actor John Barrymore, turning down an unwanted invitation

....

Darling, they've absolutely ruined your perfectly dull play.
Tallulah Bankhead, to playwright Tennessee Williams after seeing a film version of one of his plays

....

Richard Gere and Cindy Crawford – he's elastic and she's plastic.
Sandra Bernhard, comedian

....

Elizabeth Taylor looks like two small boys fighting under a mink blanket.
Mr. Blackwell

I didn't know you ever had, darling.

John Barrymore, to fellow actor Katharine Hepburn who had expressed relief at having finished a film with him and not having to act with him any more

....

She turned down the role of Helen Keller because she couldn't remember the lines.

Joan Rivers on Bo Derek

....

A buxom milkmaid reminiscent of a cow wearing a girdle, and both have the same amount of acting talent.

Mr. Blackwell, on French actor Brigitte Bardot

....

When Lauren Bacall displays her sense of humour, it's like you're witnessing a solar eclipse or some rare event.

Sally Blane, actor

....

Working with Cher was like being in a blender with an alligator.

Peter Bogdanovich, director, on working with Cher in the
1985 film, *Mask*

....

She doesn't understand the concept of Roman numerals. She thought we just fought in world war eleven.

Joan Rivers on an unknown actor

You are confusing your talent with the size of your pay check.
Marlon Brando, to fellow actor Val Kilmer

....

Her body has gone to her head.
Barbara Stanwyck on Marilyn Monroe

....

I thought I told you to wait in the car.
Tallulah Bankhead, to a man who had rushed up to her at a party,
saying, 'I haven't seen you for 41 years!'

....

There goes the famous good time that was had by all.
Bette Davis, on an unknown star of her day

....

A broad with a big future behind her.

Constance Bennett on Marilyn Monroe

....

I am able to look at my wife again and not want to hit her
because she's a woman.
Billy Wilder, after completion of *Some Like it Hot*, admitting his relief at
not having to deal with Marilyn Monroe on a daily basis

....

I am the only director who ever made two pictures with Marilyn
Monroe. Forget the Oscar. I deserve the Purple Heart.
Billy Wilder

Copulation was, I'm sure, Marilyn's way of saying thank you.

Nunnally Johnson, filmmaker, journalist and producer on Marilyn Monroe

....

Mr. Dean appears to be wearing my last year's wardrobe and using my last year's talent.

Marlon Brando, on fellow actor James Dean

....

Marilyn Monroe was smart for only ten minutes in her entire life. And that was the time it took her to sign with Twentieth Century-Fox

Anne Baxter, actor

....

He runs four miles a day and has a body like Mark Spitz. Unfortunately, he still has a face like Ernest Borgnine.

Ellen Burstyn, actor, about her husband, in the film *Same Time Next Year*

....

When it comes to acting, Joan Rivers has the range of a wart.

Stewart Klein, music, film and theatre critic

....

Necking with Marilyn Monroe is like kissing Hitler.

Tony Curtis, actor

....

Watching the non-dancing, non-singing Fred Astaire is like watching a grounded skylark.

Vincent Canby, film critic

From Poland to polo in one generation.
Arthur Caesar, screenwriter, on film producer Darryl Zanuck

....

I don't think he could direct his nephew to the bathroom.
Dyan Cannon, actor, on film director Otto Preminger

....

Earl Wilson, politician, to Tallulah Bankhead:
Have you ever been mistaken for a man?
Tallulah Bankhead:
No, darling, have you?

....

Dry and draughty, like an abandoned temple.
Truman Capote, author, on actor Greta Garbo

....

I'm just glad it'll be Clark Gable who's falling on his face and not
Gary Cooper.
Gary Cooper, actor, on his decision to turn down the leading role in
Gone With the Wind, one of the most successful films ever made

....

Hollywood glamour is a highly perishable coating which disappears after the first wash.
Gary Cooper

....

He needed willowy or boyish girls like Katharine Hepburn to
make him look what they now call macho. If I'd co-starred with
Grant or if Crawford had, we'd have eaten him for breakfast.
Bette Davis, on actor Cary Grant

Acting is the expression of a neurotic impulse. It's a bum's life. Quitting acting, that's the sign of maturity.
Marlon Brando

....

My wife was too beautiful for words, but not for arguments.
John Barrymore

....

She's a vacuum with nipples.
Otto Preminger, film director on Marilyn Monroe

....

Bob Hope is like a junkie, an applause junkie. Instead of growing old gracefully or doing something with his money, all he does is have an anniversary with the President looking on. He's a pathetic guy.
Marlon Brando

....

Faye Dunaway says she is being haunted by my mother's ghost. After her performance in *Mommie Dearest*, I can understand.
Christina Crawford, daughter of Joan Crawford whom Dunaway portrayed in *Mommie Dearest*

....

Whatever it was that this actress ever had, she still hasn't got it.
Bosley Crowther, journalist and critic, on actor Loretta Young

....

Ava Gardner to Bette Davis:
Miss Davis, I'm Ava Gardner, and I'm a great fan of yours.
Bette Davis:
Of course you are, my dear.

You were very good, Olivia. When you weren't in a scene with me you were able to keep the audience's attention.
Bette Davis, to actor Olivia de Haviland

....

Joan always cries a lot. Her tear ducts must be close to her bladder.
Bette Davis on Joan Crawford

....

Hollywood's first case of syphilis.
Bette Davis on Joan Crawford

....

I wouldn't sit on her toilet.
Bette Davis on Joan Crawford

....

When it comes to men, I heard she never turns anything down except the bedcovers.
Actor Mae West, on pin-up and actor Jayne Mansfield

....

A Marilyn Monroe gone to seed.
Dan Dailey, actor and dancer, on Jayne Mansfield

....

Miss United Dairies herself.
David Niven on Jayne Mansfield

....

Dramatic art in her opinion is knowing how to fill a sweater.
Bette Davis, on Jayne Mansfield

You shouldn't be a Governor unless you can pronounce the name of the state.

Gray Davis, Governor of California, on actor and Governor Arnold Schwarzenegger

....

I acted vulgar. Madonna *is* vulgar.

Marlene Dietrich, actor and singer

....

A day away from Tallulah is like a month in the country.

Howard Dietz, lyricist and librettist, on Tallulah Bankhead

....

Timid? As a buzz saw.

George Eels, writer, on gossip columnist, Hedda Hopper

....

He was an aloof, remote person, intent on being Cary Grant playing Cary Grant playing Cary Grant.

Frances Farmer, actor

....

All legs and hair with a mouth that could swallow the whole stadium and the hot-dog stand.

Critic, Laura Lee Davies, on singer Tina Turner

....

Tom Cruise and Nicole Kidman say their split is amicable, and they want everyone to know that after the divorce is final, their two adopted children will be returned to the props department at Universal Studios.

Tina Fey, comedian and writer

A plumber's idea of Cleopatra.
W. C. Fields, comedian and actor, on Mae West

....

Debbie Reynolds was indeed the girl next door. But only if you lived next door to a self-centred, totally driven, insecure, untruthful phoney.
Eddie Fisher, singer and ex-husband of Debbie Reynolds

....

Acting with Harvey is like acting by yourself – only worse.
Jane Fonda, actor, on actor Laurence Harvey

....

Clark Gable is the kind of guy who, if you say, 'Hiya Clark, how are you?' is stuck for an answer.
Ava Gardner, actor

....

Frank and I were always great in bed. The trouble usually started on the way to the bidet.
Ava Gardner, on her third husband, singer-actor Frank Sinatra

....

Next to privacy, the rarest thing in Hollywood is a wedding anniversary.
Gene Fowler, journalist, author and dramatist

....

In order to feel safer on his private jet, John Travolta has purchased a bomb-sniffing dog. Unfortunately for the actor, the dog came six movies too late.
Tina Fey

He looked like a half-melted rubber bulldog.

John Simon, on Walter Matthau

There are two things I would never do – climb Mount Everest and work with Val Kilmer again.

John Frankenheimer, film director

....

Hah! I always knew Frank would end up in bed with a boy!

Ava Gardner, on Frank Sinatra's marriage to actor Mia Farrow

....

I didn't know her well, but after watching her in action I didn't want to know her well.

Joan Crawford, on singer and actor Judy Garland

....

Lana Turner's a nice girl, but it's like sitting in a room with a beautiful vase.

Judy Garland, actor

....

Mel Gibson always has to be the centre of attention, otherwise he gets very unhappy and leaves.

Janeane Garofalo, comedian, actor and activist

....

He emits an air of overwhelming vanity combined with some unspecific nastiness, like a black widow spider in heat.

Roger Gellert, playwright, on comedian and actor John Cleese

....

The only thing worse than not being nominated for an Oscar would have been to be nominated and then losing to Cher. That would have been embarrassing.

Lillian Gish, actor

Any picture in which Errol Flynn is the best actor is it's own worst enemy.
Ernest Hemingway, writer

....

Burgess and I had a lot in common when we got married. I loved him and he loved him.
Paulette Goddard, on fellow actor Burgess Meredith

....

The only reason so many people showed up at his funeral was because they wanted to make sure he was dead.
Sam Goldwyn, on fellow film producer Louis B. Meyer

....

This arrogant, sour, ceremonial, pious, chauvinistic egomaniac.

Elliot Gould, actor, on comedian Jerry Lewis

....

I learned an awful lot from him by doing exactly the opposite.
Howard Hawks, on fellow film director Cecil B. De Mille

....

There's not enough money in Hollywood to lure me into making another picture with Joan Crawford. And I like money.
Sterling Hayden, actor

....

It took longer to make one of Mary Pickford's contracts than it did to make one of Mary's pictures.
Sam Goldwyn

Modesty is the artifice of actors, similar to passion in call girls.
Jackie Gleason, actor

....

A face unclouded by thought.
Lillian Hellman, playwright, on actor Norma Shearer

....

If you want to sacrifice the admiration of many men for the criticism of one, go ahead, get married.
Katharine Hepburn, actor

....

He gives her class and she gives him sex.
Katharine Hepburn, on actors and dancers Fred Astaire and Ginger Rogers

....

You had to stand in line to hate him.
Hedda Hopper, gossip columnist, on film producer Harry Cohn

....

I did not give Lee Majors his start in acting – you can't pin that on me.
Rock Hudson, actor

....

Lily Tomlin has been in and out of the closet more times than my hunting jacket.
Rock Hudson

....

Clark Gable has the best ears of our lives.
Milton Berle

His ears make him look like a taxicab with both doors open.
Howard Hughes, industrialist and film producer, on actor Clark Gable

....

Don't pay any attention to critics – don't even ignore them.
Sam Goldwyn

....

She was divinely, hysterically, insanely malevolent.
Bette Davis, on actor Theca Bara

....

A testicle with legs.
Pauline Kael, film critic on the diminutive Bob Hoskins

....

Cecil B. DeMille made small-minded pictures on a big scale.
Pauline Kael

....

She has made an acting style out of a postnasal drip.
Pauline Kael, on actor Sandy Dennis

....

I've just spent an hour talking to Tallulah for a few minutes.
Fred Keating, actor, on Tallulah Bankhead

....

He has turned almost alarmingly blond – he's gone past platinum,
he must be plutonium; his hair is coordinated with his teeth.
Pauline Kael on actor Robert Redford

....

To know him was to like him. Not to know him was to love
him.
Bert Kalmar, lyricist, on screenwiter Herman Mankowicz

Howard Hughes was the only man I ever knew who had to die to prove that he had been alive.

Walter Kane, journalist

....

Bob Hope is a funny guy but if he was drowning he couldn't ad lib 'Help!'.

Hal Kanter, writer, producer and director

....

Sincerity in Hollywood is as rare as virginity at Malibu High School.

Hal Kanter

....

The biggest bug in the manure pile.

Elia Kazan, film director, screenwriter and novelist, on Columbia Pictures president Harry Cohn

....

I watched *Titanic* when I got back home from the hospital, and cried. I knew then that my IQ had been damaged.

Stephen King, writer

....

Filming with Streisand is an experience which may have cured me of movies.

Kris Kristoferson, actor and singer-songwriter, on actor-singer Barbara Streisand

....

Kirk would be the first to tell you that he's a difficult man; I would be the second.

Burt Lancaster, on fellow actor Kirk Douglas

She looked as though butter wouldn't melt in her mouth – or anywhere else for that matter.
Elsa Lanchester, on fellow actor Maureen O'Hara

....

Ava Gardner was her customary self, as amiable as an adder.
Helen Lawrenson, journalist and magazine editor

....

George Hamilton is audibly tan.
Fran Lebowitz, author

....

Laurence Olivier is the most overrated actor on earth. Take away the wives and the looks, and you have John Gielgud.
Oscar Levant, pianist, comedian and actor

....

Fred MacMurray held on to a buck like each one was an endangered species.
Mitchell Leisen, director, art director and costume designer, on actor Fred MacMurray

....

As you know, Tom Cruise and Katie Holmes had a baby girl. It weighs seven pounds and is twenty inches long...wait, that's Tom.
David Letterman, talk-show host

....

There was no one remotely like John Houston, except, maybe, Lucifer.
Doris Lilly, gossip columnist

Doris Day is as wholesome as a bowl of cornflakes and at least as sexy.
Dwight Macdonald, film critic and writer

....

Lana Turner could give you an eyewitness account of the Crucifixion and still put you to sleep.
Herman J. Mankiewicz, screenwriter

....

The only reason he had a child was so he could meet babysitters.

David Letterman, on actor Warren Beatty

....

If people don't sit at Chaplin's feet, he goes out and stands where they are sitting.
Herman J. Mankiewicz, screenwriter, on actor and comedian Charlie Chaplin

....

I knew Doris Day before she was a virgin.
Grouch Marx, actor and comedian

....

Silicon from the knees up.
George Masters, Hollywood stylist, on actor Raquel Welch

....

I had no disagreement with Barbara Streisand. I was merely exasperated at her tendency to be a complete megalomaniac.
Walter Matthau

I once heard a producer say about Howard Hughes: 'He's entitled to his own opinion – and as many others as money can buy.'
Robert Matchup, actor

....

The curvaceous Bo Derek comes off as erotically as a Dresden doll.
The Motion Picture Guide, on the film *Bolero*

....

I gave up being serious about pictures about the time I made a film with Greer Garson and she took 127 takes to say 'no'.
Robert Mitchum, actor

....

There are three types of actress: the silly, the very silly, and Shirley MacLaine.
J. O'Rourke, writer

....

I treasure every moment that I do not see her.
Oscar Levant, on comedian Phyllis Diller

....

She looks like she combs her hair with an egg-beater.
Louella Parsons, gossip columnist, on actor Joan Collins

....

The worst and most homeliest thing to hit the screens since Liza Minelli.
John Simon, writer and critic, about Shelley Duvall

....

Wet she was a star, dry she ain't.
Joe Pasternak, film producer, on swimming film star Esther Williams

He has the attention span of a lightning bolt.

Robert Redford, on fellow actor Paul Newman

....

She's like an apple turnover that got crushed in a grocery bag on a hot day.

Camille Paglia, author and feminist, on actor Drew Barrymore

....

Johnny Depp puts the dire in director.

Edward Porter, writer

....

She stole everything but the cameras.

Actor George Raft, on Mae West's performance in her first film

....

You're a parasite for sore eyes.

Gregory Ratoff, film director

....

As a human being, Joan Crawford is a very great actress.

Nicholas Ray, film director

....

Oh my God, look at you! Anyone else hurt in the accident?

Don Rickles, comedian, to the less-than-handsome actor Ernest Borgnine

....

The man was a major comedian, which is to say that he had the compassion of an icicle, the effrontery of a carnival shrill, and the generosity of a pawnbroker.

S. J. Perelman, humorist, author and screenwriter, on Groucho Marx

Interviewing Warren Beatty is like asking a haemophiliac for a pint of blood.
Rex Reed, film critic

....

I can sing as well as Fred Astaire can act.
Burt Reynolds, actor

....

The only thing Madonna will ever do like a virgin is give birth in a stable.
Bette Midler, actor and singer

....

I can't imagine Rhett Butler chasing you for ten years.
David O. Selznick, film producer, rejecting Katharine Hepburn for the role of Scarlett O'Hara in *Gone With the Wind*

....

Frank, just make yourself at home and hit somebody.
Don Rickles, to singer and actor Frank Sinatra

....

I would rather drink latex paint than be in a movie with Steven Seagal.

Henry Rollins, actor, comedian and singer

....

The insufferably smug and woodchuck-cheeked Minnie Driver proffers what the French call a *tête à gifler* – a face begging to be slapped.
Critic John Simon

They say Tom Mix rides as if he's part of the horse, but they don't say which part.
Robert Sherwood, playwright and screenwriter

....

Most of the time he sounds like he has a mouth full of toilet paper.
Rex Reed, on actor Marlon Brando

....

Jack Lemmon has a gift for butchering good parts while managing to look intelligent, thus constituting Hollywood's abiding answer to the theatre.
Wilfred Sheed, writer

....

The only real talent Miss Day possesses is that of being absolutely sanitary: her personality untouched by human emotions, her brow unclouded by human thought, her form unsmudged by the slightest evidence of femininity.
John Simon, on actor Doris Day

....

Her work, if that is the word for it, always consists chiefly of a dithering, blithering, neurotic coming apart at the seams – an acting style that is really a nervous breakdown in slow motion.
John Simon, on actor Diane Keaton

....

It proves what they always say: give the public what they want to see, and they'll come out for it.
Red Skelton, radio, television and film star, on the crowds at Harry Cohn's funeral

I've got three words for him: Am. A. Teur.
Charlie Sheen, on fellow actor Colin Farrell

....

The sad thing is that he has consistently put his very real talent to the task of glorifying his imaginary genius.
John Simon, on actor and film director Orson Welles

....

Well at least he has finally found his true love…what a pity he can't marry himself.
Frank Sinatra, singer and actor, on actor Robert Redford

....

Not in this lifetime. Why? Because I'm the only one she hasn't done it to.
Sharon Stone, on being told that Madonna has said she wants to kiss her

....

An appalling man and, even more unforgivingly, an appalling actor.
Robert Stevens, film director, on actor Laurence Harvey

....

He is to acting what Liberace was to pumping iron.

Rex Reed, on actor Sylvester Stallone

....

He got a reputation as a great actor by just thinking hard about the next line.
King Vidor, film director, on Gary Cooper

In one scene in *Jinxed* I have to hit her in the face and I thought, we could save some money in sound effects here.

Ken Wahl, actor, on working with Bette Midler

....

There are times when Richard Gere has the warm effect of a wind tunnel at dawn.

David Thompson, writer

....

Elizabeth Taylor isn't spoiled. I have often seen her pour her own champagne for breakfast.

Mike Todd, theatre and film producer, and third husband of Elizabeth Taylor

....

I thank God that neither I nor any member of my family will ever be so hard up that we have to work for Otto Preminger.

Lana Turner, actor

....

The softest thing about him is his front teeth.

Damon Runyan, writer, on film producer Harry Cohn

....

A passionate amoeba.

David Susskind, film producer, on Tony Curtis

....

A cross between an aardvark and an albino rat.

John Simon, on Barbara Streisand

....

He's the type of man who will end up dying in his own arms.

Mamie van Doreen, actor, on Warren Beatty

In some of his last movies, Errol Flynn had to play himself. Unfortunately, the role was beyond his abilities.

Jack L. Warner, president of Warner Brothers

....

They say Louis B. Mayer is his own worst enemy. Not while I'm still alive.

Jack L. Warner

....

The only way I could force myself to kiss Midler on-camera was to pretend that I was kissing my dog.

Ken Wahl on Bette Midler

....

She's the kind of woman who climbed the ladder of success – wrong by wrong.

Mae West, on fellow screen siren Jean Harlow

....

I welcome him like I welcome cold sores.

Paula Abdul, singer, on her fellow *American Idol* judge, Simon Cowell

....

What do you mean heart attack? You've got to have a heart before you can have an attack.

Billy Wilder, film director, on actor Peter Sellers

....

I approached reading his review the way some people anticipate anal warts.

Roseanne Barr, on the prospect of being reviewed by critic Ray Richmond

Tallulah talked so ceaselessly that you had to make a reservation five minutes ahead to get a word in.

Earl Wilson, newspaper columnist, on Tallulah Bankhead

....

Can you imagine Simon as a kid? His imaginary friends probably didn't want to play with him.

Paula Abdul on Simon Cowell

....

My attitude about Hollywood is that I wouldn't walk across the street to pull one of those executives out of the snow if he was bleeding to death. Not unless I was paid for it.

James Woods, actor

....

The nicest thing I can say about Frances Farmer is that she is unbearable.

William Wyler, film director

....

They call her Katharine of Arrogance.

Actor Estelle Winwood on Katharine Hepburn

....

Milton Berle has done everyone's act. He's a parrot with skin on.

Fred Allen

....

Every dude has had a fantasy about Jessica Simpson. Here's mine: Jessica, hold your sister Ashlee so I can kick her in the throat.

Dave Attell, comedian

He has Van Gogh's ear for music.

Billy Wilder, on actor Cliff Osmond whose film role called upon him to sing

....

I'm only upset that I'm not a widow.

Roseanne Barr, comedian, following her divorce from actor and writer Tom Arnold

....

The closest thing to Roseanne Barr's singing the national anthem was my cat being neutered.

Johnny Carson

....

He's a male chauvinistic piglet.

Betty Friedan, writer and feminist, on Groucho Marx

....

Valentine's Day is the day you should be with the one you love the most. I understand Simon Cowell spent the day alone.

Jay Leno

....

Television is to news what bumper stickers are to philosophy.

Richard Nixon, 37th president

....

Who picks your clothes? Stevie Wonder?

Don Rickles to David Letterman

....

The trouble with Tony Curtis is that he's interested only in tight pants and wide billing.

Billy Wilder

The fastest way to a man's heart is through his chest.
Roseanne Barr

....

Why are you always speeding? It's not like you've got people holding their breath till you get there.

Don Rickles to David Letterman

Literature

Alexander Woollcott, signing a first edition of one of his books:
Ah what is so rare as a Woollcott first edition?
Franklin P. Adams:
A Woollcott second edition.
An exchange between writer Alexander Woollcott and journalist,
Franklin P. Adams

....

I have only been mildly bored.
Gertrude Atherton, after a lengthy debate with fellow writer Ambrose
Bierce

....

She is a combination of Little Nell and Lady Macbeth.
Alexander Woollcott, writer, on poet and wit Dorothy Parker

....

From the moment I picked your book up until I laid it down I
was convulsed with laughter. Some day I intend reading it.
Groucho Marx on a book by S. J. Perelman

....

I thought there could only be two worse writers than Stephen
Crane, namely two Stephen Cranes.
Ambrose Bierce, journalist and writer

....

I guess Gore left the country because he felt he was under-
appreciated here. I have news for him; people who actually read
his books will under-appreciate him everywhere.
Truman Capote, author, on literary rival Gore Vidal

Longfellow is to poetry what the barrel organ is to music.

Van Wyck Brooks, critic, on poet Henry Wadsworth Longfellow

....

The smartest of alecs.

Heywood Broun, journalist, on writer Alexander Woollcott

....

This is not a novel to be tossed aside lightly. It should be thrown with great force.

Dorothy Parker

....

That's not writing, that's typing.

Truman Capote on Jack Kerouac's book *On the Road*

....

Jacqueline Susann looks like a truck driver in drag.

Truman Capote on the best-selling author

....

The covers of this book are too far apart.

Ambrose Bierce

....

He was a great friend of mine. Well, as much as you could be a friend of his, unless you were a 14-year-old nymphet.

Truman Capote, on writer William Faulkner

....

He was humane but not human.

E. E. Cummings on fellow poet Ezra Pound

Tennyson is a beautiful half of a poet.

Ralph Waldo Emerson, essayist and poet, on poet Alfred, Lord Tennyson

....

Is Wordsworth a bell with a wooden tongue?

Ralph Waldo Emerson, on poet William Wordsworth

....

Every drop of blood in that man's veins has eyes that look downward.

Ralph Waldo Emerson, American philosopher and poet, on American politician Daniel Webster,

....

Even those who call Mr. Faulkner our greatest literary sadist do not fully appreciate him, for it is not merely his characters who have to run the gauntlet but also his readers.

Clifton Fadiman, author and television personality, on writer William Faulkner

....

I found nothing really wrong with this autobiography except poor choice of subject.

Clifton Fadiman, on Gertrude Stein's *Everybody's Autobiography*

....

Miss Stein was a past master in making nothing happen very slowly.

Clifton Fadiman, on writer Gertrude Stein

....

One of the nicest old ladies I have ever met.

William Faulkner, on fellow author, Henry James

A hack writer who would have been considered fourth rate in Europe, who tried out a few of the old proven 'sure-fire' literary skeletons with sufficient local color to intrigue the superficial and the lazy.

William Faulkner on fellow author Mark Twain

....

Half song thrush, half alligator.

Ralph Waldo Emerson on poet Walt Whitman

....

Always willing to lend a helping hand to the one above him.

F. Scott Fitzgerald, on fellow author Ernest Hemingway

....

To me, Pound remains the exquisite showman minus the show.

Ben Hecht, writer, on Ezra Pound

....

She was incredibly ugly, uglier than almost anyone I had ever met. A thin, withered creature, she sat hunched in her chair, in her heavy tweed suit and her thick lisle stockings, impregnable and indifferent. She had a huge nose, a dark moustache, and her dark-dyed hair was combed into absurd bangs over her forehead.

Otto Friedrich, journalist, on writer Alice B. Toklas

....

A man must be a very great genius to make up for being such a loathsome human being.

Martha Gelhorn, journalist, on Ernest Hemingway

....

The greatest mind ever to stay in prep school.

Writer Norman Mailer, on writer J. D. Salinger

Mr. Fitzgerald – I believe that is how he spells his name – seems to believe that plagiarism begins at home.

Zelda Fitzgerald, reviewing her husband F. Scott Fitzgerald's novel *The Beautiful and the Damned*

....

Thank you for sending me a copy of your book; I'll waste no time in reading it.

Moses Hadas, classical scholar

....

Jane Austen's books, too, are absent from this library. Just that one omission alone would make a fairly good library out of a library that hadn't a book in it.

Mark Twain

....

For my part, I can rarely tell whether his characters are making love or playing tennis.

Joseph Kraft, journalist, on William Faulkner

....

It is like making love to a 300 lb woman. Once she gets on top, it's all over. Fall in love or be asphyxiated.

Norman Mailer, on reading a long novel by Thomas Wolfe

....

What an old covered wagon she is.

F. Scott Fitzgerald on Gertrude Stein

....

Every word she writes is a lie, including 'and' and 'the'.

Mary McCarthy, author, on playwright Lilian Hellman

Jacqueline Susann looks like a truck driver in drag.

Truman Capote on the best-selling author

To me, Edgar Allen Poe's prose is unreadable – like Jane Austen's. No, there's a difference. I could read his prose on a salary, but not Jane's.
Mark Twain

....

A little emasculated mass of inanity.
Theodore Roosevelt, 26th President, on novelist Henry James

....

Jane Austen's novels, which strangely retain their hold on the public taste, are tedious to those who dare to think for themselves.
Kate Sanborn, author and teacher

....

A Republican housewife from Kansas with all the prejudices.
Gore Vidal, on Truman Capote

....

She preserved to the age of 56 that contempt for ideas which is normal among boys and girls of 15.
Odell Shepard, professor, poet and politician, on writer Louisa May Alcott

....

In conversation he is even duller than in writing, if that is possible.
Juliana Smith, wife of mid-19th century mayor of New York, on lexicographer Noah Webster

....

A village explainer. Excellent if you were a village, but if you were not, not.
Gertrude Stein, writer, on Ezra Pound

In her last days, she resembled a spoiled pear.
Gore Vidal on Gertrude Stein

....

The profession of book-writing makes horse racing seem like a solid, stable business.
John Steinbeck, author

....

Valley of the Dolls – for the reader who has put away comic books, but isn't ready for editorials in the *Daily News*.
Gloria Steinem, journalist and feminist, reviewing Jacqueline Susann's novel

....

Walt Whitman was not only eager to talk about himself but reluctant to have the conversation stray from the subject for far too long.
Henry D. Thoreau, writer and philosopher

....

Once you've put one of his books down, you simply can't pick it up again.
Mark Twain on Henry James

....

If a person is not talented enough to be a novelist, not smart enough to be a lawyer, and his hands are too shaky to perform operations, he becomes a journalist.
Norman Mailer

....

Truman Capote has made lying an art. A minor art.
Gore Vidal

Writing criticism is to writing fiction and poetry as hugging the shore is to sailing in the open sea.

John Updike, novelist, on critics

....

What other culture could have produced someone like Hemingway and *not* seen the joke?

Gore Vidal on Ernest Hemingway

....

If he were to write about an Orphan Princess who lost a peanut, he would feel obliged to make somebody snuffle over it.

Mark Twain, on author and poet Bret Harte

....

I always said little Truman Capote had a voice so high it could only be detected by bats.

Tennessee Williams, playwright

....

His style has the desperate jauntiness of an orchestra fiddling away for dear life on a sinking ship.

Edmund Wilson, writer and critic, on British writer Evelyn Waugh

....

Reading Proust is like bathing in someone else's dirty water.

Alexander Woollcott

....

Truman Capote's death was a good career move.

Gore Vidal

Music

Anton Bruckner wrote the same symphony nine times, trying to get it right. He failed.
Edward Abbey, author

....

I can't listen to that much Wagner. I start getting the urge to conquer Poland.
Woody Allen, comedian, actor and film director

....

A human ashtray with duvet-sized bags between his hallucino-genic blue eyes.
Tina Brown, journalist, on French singer-songwriter Serge Gainsbourg

....

I was a fan of hers back when she was popular.
Mariah Carey, when asked if she was a fan of fellow singer Madonna

....

If life was fair, Elvis would be alive and all the impersonators would be dead.
Johnny Carson, talk-show host

....

Listening to the Fifth Symphony of Ralph Vaughan Williams is like staring at a cow for 45 minutes.
Aaron Copeland, composer

....

Jazz: Music invented for the torture of imbeciles.
Henry van Dyke, clergyman and educator

Opera is when a guy gets stabbed in the back and, instead of bleeding, he sings.

Ed Gardner, actor, writer and director

....

I don't like country music, but I don't mean to denigrate those who do; and for the people who like country music, denigrate means 'put down'.

Bob Newhart, comedian

....

Bambi on testosterone.

Owen Gleiberman, film critic, on singer and musician Prince

....

Mariah Carey says she believes there is an orchestrated conspiracy by a large number of people to keep her career and record sales down. I think that's called the public.

Jay Leno, talk-show host

....

Tell me, George, if you had to do it all over, would you fall in love with yourself again?

Oscar Levant, pianist, comedian and actor, to composer George Gershwin

....

Mick Jagger is now at that awkward age between being a Stone and passing one.

Jay Leno

The easiest way for you to lose 10 lbs is to just take off your wig.

Madonna, in a note to fellow singer Elton John

....

Elvis transcends his talent to the point of dispensing with it altogether.

Grail Marcus, writer, on singer Elvis Presley

....

He sang like a hinge.

Ethel Merman, singer, on composer Cole Porter

....

She ought to be arrested for loitering in front of an orchestra.

Actor Bette Midler, on singer Helen Reddy

....

Her voice sounded like an eagle being goosed.

Ralph Novak, guitar-maker, on singer-artist Yoko Ono

....

Sixty-year-old Barry Manilow is going in for hip surgery this month. That's three words you've never heard before in the same sentence: Barry, Manilow and hip.

Jay Leno

....

Michael Jackson's album was only called 'Bad' because there wasn't enough room on the sleeve for 'Pathetic'.

Prince

I'm so glad Courtney Love is here; I left my crack in my other purse.

Sarah Silverman, comedian and actor

....

Rock star Adam Ant has pleaded guilty to hitting a man during a bar fight. If Adam Ant really did attack the man, it would be his first hit since 1986.

Conan O'Brien, talk-show host

....

I hope the next time she crosses a street four blind guys come along driving cars.

Frank Sinatra, singer and actor, on his biographer Kitty Kelley

....

What are you doing here? Is the war over?

Comedian Don Rickles to Bob Hope, famous for entertaining the troops during World War II

....

She's like a breast with a boom box.

Judy Tenuta, comedian, on Madonna

....

His kind of music is deplorable, a rancid-smelling aphrodisiac.

Frank Sinatra, on Elvis Presley

Nationalities & Places

New Yorkers like to boast that if you can survive in New York, you can survive anywhere. But if you can survive anywhere, why live in New York?
Edward Abbey, author

....

I once spent a year in Philadelphia; I think it was a Sunday.
W. C. Fields, comedian and actor

....

Canada is a country so square that even the female impersonators are women.
Richard Brenner, film director

....

Miami is where neon goes to die.
Lenny Bruce, comedian

....

I don't even know what street Canada is on.
Al Capone, gangster

....

All Englishmen talk as if they've got a bushel of plums stuck in their throats, and then after swallowing them get constipated from the pips.
W. C. Fields

....

If you're going to America, bring your own food.
Fran Lebowitz, author

Of course, America had often been discovered before Columbus, but it had always been hushed up.
Oscar Wilde

....

The trouble with America is that there are too many wide, open spaces surrounded by teeth.
Charles Luckman, businessman and architect

....

Nothing is wrong with California that a rise in the ocean level wouldn't cure.
Ross MacDonald, crime writer

....

We Americans have always considered Hollywood, at best, a sinkhole of depraved venality.
David Mamet, playwright, screenwriter and film director

....

An Iranian moderate is one who has run out of ammunition.

Henry Kissinger, political scientist and Secretary of State

....

It's going to be a great country when they finish unpacking it.
Andrew H. Malcolm, US journalist, on Canada

....

No one ever went broke underestimating the taste of the American public.
H. L. Mencken, writer

Hollywood is a trip through a sewer in a glass-bottom boat.
Wilson Mizner, playwright

....

It has been reported that Spain is the number one consumer of cocaine in the world. Apparently, Spain narrowly beat Kate Moss.
Conan O'Brien, talk-show host

....

Hollywood is a carnival where there are no concessions…a sewer, with service from the Ritz Carlton.
Wilson Mizner

....

Hollywood is a place that attracts people with massive holes in their souls.
Julia Phillips, author and film producer

....

One thing I will say about the Germans, they are always perfectly willing to give somebody's land to somebody else.
Will Rogers, comedian and social commentator

....

Very little is known of the Canadian country since it is rarely visited by anyone but the Queen and illiterate sport fishermen.
P. J. O'Rourke, writer

....

The American male doesn't mature until he has exhausted all other possibilities.
Wilfred Sheed, writer

The trouble with Oakland (California) is that when you get there, it's there.

Gertrude Stein, writer

....

I've been to Canada, and I've always gotten the impression that I could take the country over in about two days.

Jon Stewart, television host and political satirist

....

France is a country where the money falls apart in your hands but you can't tear the toilet paper.

Billy Wilder, film director

....

Hollywood: a place where they shoot too many pictures and not enough actors.

Walter Winchell, newspaper and radio commentator

....

America is one long expectoration.

Oscar Wilde writer and poet

Politics

He told us he was going to take crime out of the streets. He did. He took it into the damn White House.

Ralph Abernathy, Civil Rights leader, on 37th president, Richard Nixon

....

Nixon impeached himself. He gave us Gerald Ford as his revenge.

Bella Abzug, Congresswoman, on Richard Nixon

....

A pin-stripin' polo-playin' umbrella-totin' Ivy-Leaguer, born with a silver spoon so far in his mouth that you couldn't get it out with a crowbar.

Bill Baxley, politician, on 43rd President George W. Bush

....

In my lifetime, we've gone from Eisenhower to George W. Bush. We've gone from John F. Kennedy to Al Gore. Now if that is evolution, I believe that in twelve years, we're gonna be voting for plants.

Lewis Black, comedian

....

Bill Clinton's foreign policy experience is pretty much confined to having had breakfast once at the International House of Pancakes.

Pat Buchanan, political commentator

Bill Clinton is a man who thinks international affairs means dating a girl from out of town.

Tom Clancy, author

....

I met Dick Cheney the other night. I've never stood that close to evil.

Lewis Black

....

Poet and wit, Dorothy Parker on learning that President Calvin Coolidge had just died:

How can they tell?

....

He is a man of his most recent word.

William F. Buckley, author and commentator, on President Lyndon B. Johnson

....

Nixon is a man who has the morals of a private detective.

William S. Burroughs, writer, on Richard Nixon

....

The hustler from Chicago.

George H. W. Bush, 41st President, on civil rights leader Jesse Jackson

....

Fox News gives you both sides of every story – the President's side and the Vice-President's side.

Stephen Colbert, political satirist

Ronald Reagan doesn't dye his hair, he bleaches his face.
Johnny Carson, talk-show host

....

We did not conceive it possible that even Mr. Lincoln would produce a paper so slipshod, so loose-joined, so puerile, not alone in literary construction, but in its ideas, its sentiments, its grasp. He has outdone himself.
Chicago Times, on 16th president, Abraham Lincoln's Gettysburg Address

....

I worship the quicksand he walks in.

Art Buchwald, humorist, on Richard Nixon

....

Dorothy Parker on hearing that politician and playwright Clare Boothe Luce was apparently kind to her inferiors:
Wherever does she find them?

....

Hoover, if elected, will do one thing that is almost incomprehensible to the human mind: he will make a great man out of Coolidge.
Clarence Darrow, lawyer, during the presidential campaign of 1928

....

Nixon's motto was, if two wrongs don't make a right, try three.
Norman Cousins, journalist, on Richard Nixon

Young girl to Calvin Coolidge, the 30th president famous for not talking much:

Oh, Mr. President, Poppa says if I can get three words out of you he will buy me a fur coat.

Coolidge's reply:

You lose.

....

Walter Mondale has all the charisma of a speed bump.

Will Durst, political satirist, on the presidential candidate

....

Bush doesn't know the names of countries, he doesn't know the names of foreign leaders, he can't even find the Earth on a globe.

Doug Ferrari, comedian, on George W. Bush

....

When I was president, I said I was a Ford, not a Lincoln. Well what we have now is a convertible Dodge.

Gerald Ford, on 42nd president, Bill Clinton

....

When I was a boy, I was told anybody could become President of the United States; I'm beginning to believe it.

Clarence Darrow

....

They don't have a page that broad.

Gennifer Flowers, alleged mistress of Bill Clinton on why Hilary Clinton could not 'bare her butt in any magazine.'

He doesn't dye his hair – he's just prematurely orange.

Gerald Ford, on 40th President Ronald Reagan

....

Hubert Humphrey talks so fast that listening to him is like trying to read *Playboy* magazine with your wife turning the pages.

Barry Goldwater, senator

....

Garfield has shown that he is not possessed of the backbone of an angleworm.

Ulysses S. Grant, 18th president, on James A. Garfield, 20th president

....

Dan Quayle is more stupid than Ronald Reagan put together.

Matt Groening, animator

....

Those who stand for nothing fall for anything.

Alexander Hamilton, US Founding Father

....

If ignorance goes to $40 a barrel, I want drilling rights to George Bush's head.

Jim Hightower, journalist

....

If he were any dumber, he'd be a tree.

Senator Barry Goldwater, on politician William Scott

....

I have never seen... so slippery, so disgusting a candidate.

Nat Hentoff, newspaper columnist and critic, on Bill Clinton

We need a President who's fluent in at least one language.
Buck Henry, actor and film director, on George W. Bush

....

Talk is cheap – except when Congress does it.
Cullen Hightower, writer

....

Filthy Story-Teller, Despot, Liar, Thief, Braggart, Buffoon, Usurper, Monster, Ignoramus Abe, Old Scoundrel, Perjurer, Robber, Swindler, Tyrant, Field-Butcher, Land-Pirate.

Writer for *Harper's Weekly*, on Abraham Lincoln

....

Avoid all needle drugs – the only dope worth shooting is Richard Nixon.
Abby Hoffman, political activist

....

If he wants to do his country a favour, he'll stay over there.
Barry Goldwater, on Richard Nixon's trip to China

....

Dewey has thrown his diaper into the ring.
Harold L. Ickes on the young presidential candidate Thomas E. Dewey

....

Sir Richard the Chicken-Hearted.
Hubert Humphrey on Richard Nixon

Every politician should have been born an orphan and remain a bachelor.

Lady Bird Johnson, wife of 36th president, Lyndon B. Johnson

....

The trouble with Senator Long is that he is suffering from halitosis of the intellect. That's presuming Emperor Long has an intellect.

Harold L. Ickes, politician, on Governor of Louisiana Huey Long

....

Do you realize the responsibility I carry? I'm the only person between (Richard) Nixon and the White House.

John F. Kennedy, during the 1960 presidential campaign

....

Ted Kennedy said Iraq is George W. Bush's Vietnam. Which is very unfair. There is a huge difference. Bush knew how to get out of Vietnam.

Jay Leno, talk-show host

....

He is your typical smiling, brilliant, back-stabbing, southern nut-cutter.

Lane Kirkland, union leader, on 39th president, Jimmy Carter

....

Jerry Ford is a nice guy, but he played too much football with his helmet off.

Lyndon B. Johnson

....

Instead of giving a politician the keys to the city, it might be better to change the locks.

Doug Larson, journalist

George W. Bush: this is a guy who couldn't find oil in Texas.

Al Franken, senator

You and I were long friends; you are now my enemy, and I am Yours, B. Franklin.

US Founding Father Benjamin Franklin in a letter to publisher William Strahan

....

You get 15 democrats in a room, and you get 20 opinions.

Patrick Leahy, senator

....

You can always tell a Harvard man but you can't tell them much.

Dwight D. Eisenhower, 34th president, on 35th president, John F. Kennedy

....

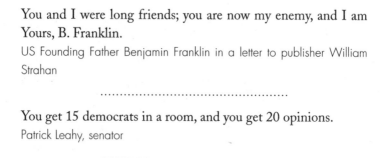

The reason there are so few female politicians is that it is too much trouble to put make-up on two faces.

Maureen Murphy, politician

....

His argument is as thin as the homeopathic soup that was made by boiling the shadow of a pigeon that had been starved to death.

Abraham Lincoln, on presidential rival Stephen A. Douglas

....

My brother Bob doesn't want to be in government – he promised Dad he'd go straight.

John F. Kennedy

The Wizard of Ooze.
John F. Kennedy, on Senator Everett Dirksen who was renowned for his overblown oratory

....

The only difference between the Democrats and the Republicans is that the Democrats allow the poor to be corrupt, too.
Oscar Levant, pianist, comedian and actor

....

He looks as though he's been weaned on a pickle.
Alice Roosevelt Longworth, daughter of 26th president, Theodore Roosevelt, on Calvin Coolidge

....

No woman has ever so comforted the distressed – or distressed the comfortable.
Clare Boothe Luce on Eleanor Roosevelt, First Lady from 1933–1945

....

I believe that Ronald Reagan can make this country what it once was – an Arctic region covered with ice.
Steve Martin, actor and comedian

....

He's nothing more than a well meaning baboon.
General George B. McCellan, American Civil War soldier, on Abraham Lincoln

....

The enviably attractive nephew who sings an Irish ballad for the company and then winsomely disappears before the table clearing and dishwashing begin.
Lyndon B. Johnson, on John F. Kennedy

I would like to apologize for referring to George W. Bush as a 'deserter'. What I meant to say is that George W. Bush is a deserter, an election thief, a drunk driver, a WMD liar and a functional illiterate. And he poops his pants.

Michael Moore, filmmaker

....

The battle for the mind of Ronald Reagan was like the trench warfare of World War I: never have so many fought so hard for such barren territory.

Peggy Noonan, writer

....

You can put lipstick on a pig... it's still a pig.

Barack Obama, 44th president in a thinly veiled reference to vice presidential candidate, Sarah Palin

....

He wouldn't commit himself to the time from a hatful of watches.

Westbrook Pegler, journalist, on 31st president, Herbert Hoover

....

We make fun of George W. Bush, but this morning he was at work bright and early. Okay, he was early.

Jay Leno

....

As he rose like a rocket, so he fell like a stick.

Thomas Paine, on statesman and political theorist Edmund Burke

He is racist, he's homophobic, he's xenophobic, and he's sexist. He's the perfect Republican candidate.

Bill Press, journalist, on Republican presidential candidate
Pat Buchanan

....

An empty suit that goes to funerals and plays golf.
Ross Perot, businessman and presidential candidate, on Vice President
Dan Quayle

....

Politics is supposed to be the second oldest profession. I have
come to realise that it bears a very close resemblance to the first.
Ronald Reagan

....

It has been the political career of this man to begin with hypoc-
risy, proceed with arrogance, and finish with contempt.
US Founding Father Thomas Paine, on 2nd president, John Adams

....

They never open their mouths without subtracting from the sum
of human knowledge.
Thomas Brackett Reed, Speaker of the US House of Representatives, on
orators in the US House of Representatives

....

He can't help it – he was born with a silver foot in his mouth.
Ann Richards, Governor of Texas, on George W. Bush

The trouble with political jokes is that very often they get elected.

Will Rogers, comedian and social commentator

....

A conservative is one who admires radicals centuries after they're dead.

Leo Rosten, teacher, journalist and screenwriter

....

Washington could not tell a lie; Nixon could not tell the truth; Reagan cannot tell the difference.

Mort Sahl, comedian and actor

....

He's a Boy Scout with a hormone imbalance.

Kevin Phillips, political commentator, on George W. Bush

....

A working man voting for Ronald Reagan is like a chicken voting for Colonel Sanders.

Paul Sarbanes, senator

....

I am not a member of any organized political party. I am a Democrat.

Will Rogers

....

If I owned Texas and Hell, I would rent out Texas and live in Hell.

Philip H. Sheridan, Union general in the American Civil War

The worst thing a little acid could do to Tricia Nixon is to turn her into a merely delightful person instead of a grinning robot.
Grace Slick, singer with Jefferson Airplane, on Richard Nixon's daughter

....

If the Republicans will stop telling lies about the Democrats, we will stop telling the truth about them.
Adlai Stevenson, Governor of Illinois and Ambassador to the United Nations

....

Nixon is the kind of politician who would cut down a redwood tree and then mount the stump to make a speech for conversation.
Adlai Stevenson, on Richard Nixon

....

A fool and his money are soon elected.
Will Rogers

....

Truman proves the old adage that any man can become President of the United States.
Norman Thomas, socialist and presidential candidate, on 33rd president, Harry S. Truman

....

A triumph of the embalmer's art.

Gore Vidal on Ronald Reagan

....

President Nixon was so crooked that he needed servants to help him screw his pants on every morning.
Hunter S. Thompson, writer, journalist and political commentator

Reagan won because he ran against Jimmy Carter, if he'd run unopposed he would have lost.

Mort Sahl on Ronald Reagan

....

Such a little man could not have made so big a depression.

Norman Thomas, on Herbert Hoover

....

You look at George W. and you realize that some people are born great, some achieve greatness, and some get it as a graduation gift.

Robin Williams, on George W. Bush

....

He has a bungalow mind.

Woodrow Wilson, 28th president, on 29th president, Warren Harding

....

About all I can say for the United States Senate is that it opens with a prayer and closes with an investigation.

Will Rogers

....

A nonentity with side whiskers.

Woodrow Wilson, on 21st president, Chester A. Arthur

....

You want a friend in Washington? Get a dog.

Harry S. Truman

He's proof that there's life after death.
Mort Sahl, on Ronald Reagan

....

When Bob Dole does smile, he looks as if he's just evicted a widow.
Mike Royko, newspaper columnist

....

He inherited some good instincts from his Quaker forebears, but by diligent hard work, he overcame them.
James Reston, journalist, on Richard Nixon

....

The Eichmann trial taught the world the banality of evil; now Nixon is teaching the world the evil of banality.
J. F. Stone, writer, on Richard Nixon

....

Why this fellow don't know any more about politics than a pig knows about Sunday.
Harry S. Truman, on President Dwight D. Eisenhower

....

Ninety eight per cent of the adults in this country are decent, hardworking, honest Americans. It's the other lousy two per cent that get all the publicity. But then, we elected them.

Lily Tomlin, actor

Reader, suppose you were an idiot; and suppose you were a member of Congress; but I repeat myself.

Mark Twain, author, on the US Congress

....

People say satire is dead. It's not dead; it's alive and living in the White House.

Actor Robin Williams, on Ronald Reagan

....

I think Nancy does most of his talking; you'll notice that she never drinks water when Ronnie speaks.

Robin Williams, on Ronald Reagan

Sport

Howard Cosell was gonna be a boxer when he was a kid, only they couldn't find a mouthpiece big enough.
Muhammad Ali, world heavyweight boxing champion

....

Reporter: What would you do if you retired?
Charles Barclay, basketball star: If push came to shove, I could lose all self-respect and become a reporter.

....

Although golf was originally restricted to wealthy, overweight Protestants, today it's open to anybody who owns hideous clothing.
Dave Barry, author and newspaper columnist

....

I've seen George Foreman shadow boxing, and the shadow won.
Muhammad Ali

....

He doesn't know the meaning of the word 'fear.' Of course, if you look at his grades, you'll realize that he doesn't know the meaning of a lot of words.
Bobby Bowden, college football coach, on a fellow player

....

Martina was so far in the closet that she was in danger of being a garment bag.
Rita Mae Brown, novelist and activist, on tennis player Martina Navratilova

. . . .

I've seen George Foreman shadow boxing, and the shadow won.

. . . .

Muhammad Ali

It's good that Mike Tyson's been granted parole. More steps must be taken like this to make our prisons safer places.
Greg Cote, journalist

Sonny Lison's so ugly that when he cries the tears run down the back of his head.

Muhammad Ali

I don't want to catch anything. That thing has been passed around more often than Paris Hilton.
Theo Epstein, baseball general manager, refusing to handle the World Series trophy

Ken Norton: My wife just had a baby.
Joe Frazier: Congratulations! Whose baby is it?
Frazier, heavyweight boxing champion, to boxing rival Norton

Me and Jake LaMotta grew up in the same neighbourhood. You wanna know how popular Jake was? When we played hide-and-seek, nobody ever looked for LaMotta.
Rocky Graziano, boxer, on his legendary competitor

In the next issue of *Cosmopolitan*, Howard Cosell will be the centrefold with his vital organ covered – his mouth.
Burt Reynolds, on sports commentator, Howard Cosell

Show me a good loser, and I'll show you a loser.
Vince Lombardi, football coach

....

What's the penalty for killing a photographer – one stroke or two?
Davis Love III, professional golfer

....

I don't like that Hubert H. Humphrey Metrodome. It's a shame a great guy like Humphrey had to be named after it.
Billy Martin, baseball player and manager, on the Minneapolis sports stadium

....

Promoter Don King took a ride on a dogsled. It was so cold, he had his hands in his own pockets.
Chris Myers, sports broadcaster

....

I don't know what it is, but I can't look at Hulk Hogan and believe that he's the end result of millions and millions of years of evolution.
Jim Murray, sportswriter, on wrestler Hulk Hogan

....

Have you heard of that part of the body called a spine? Get one!
Andy Roddick, tennis player, to a tennis umpire

....

You've just one problem; you stand too close to the ball – after you've hit it.
Sam Snead, golfer, to an unnamed golfer

Hockey is a sport for white men. Basketball is a sport for black men. Golf is a sport for white men dressed like black pimps.
Tiger Woods, golfer

....

No word yet if Kournikova will sue, but it would be the only court appearance she'd actually have a chance of winning.
Ken Rudolph, baseball player, on fake topless pictures of Anna Kournikova that appeared in *Penthouse*

....

What other problems do you have besides being unemployed, a moron, and a dork?
John McEnroe, to a spectator at one of his matches

....

Tommy Morrison proved that he is an ambidextrous boxer. He can get knocked out with either hand.
Bert Sugar, boxing writer

Theatre

I understand your new play is full of single entendre.
George S. Kaufman, theatre producer, director and playwright, to
playwright Howard Dietz

....

When Mr. Wilbur calls his play *Halfway to Hell* he underestimates the distance.
Brooks Atkinson, theatre critic

....

Perfectly Scandalous was one of those plays in which all the actors, unfortunately, enunciated very clearly.
Robert Benchley, newspaper columnist

....

It opened at 8.40 sharp and closed at 10.40 dull.
Heywood Broun, journalist

....

Miss Strozzi had the temerity to wear as truly horrible a gown as I have ever seen on the American stage…had she not luckily been strangled by a member of the cast while disporting this garment, I should have fought my way to the stage and done her in myself.
Poet and wit Dorothy Parker on actor Kay Strozzi starring in the play *The Silent Witness*

....

Go to the Martin Beck Theater and watch Katharine Hepburn run the whole gamut of emotions from A to B.
Dorothy Parker on actor Katharine Hepburn in *The Lake*, on Broadway

Mrs. Patrick Campbell, to the producer of George Bernard Shaw's play, *Pygmalion*, in which she was starring on Broadway:

Always remember, Mr. Froham, that I am an artist.

Charles Frohman, theatrical producer:

Your secret's safe with me.

....

Excuse me, my leg has gone to sleep. Do you mind if I join it.

Alexander Woollcott, writer, to a boring young actor

....

Actor, Dustin Farnum:

I've never been better! In the last act yesterday, I had the audience glued to their seats.

Oliver Herford, British-born American writer:

How clever of you to think of it.

....

Frank Rich and John Simon are the syphilis and gonorrhea of the theatre.

David Mamet, playwright, on the two powerful theatre critics

....

It was a bad play saved by a bad performance.

George S. Kaufman, on the performance of Gertrude Lawrence in a play called *Skylark*

....

The triumph of sugar over diabetes.

George Jean Nathan, drama critic, on author and dramatist J. M. Barrie

....

Watching your performance from the rear of the house. Wish you were here.

George S. Kaufman, to actor William Gaxton

The scenery was beautiful, but the actors got in front of it.
Alexander Woollcott

....

He always praises the first production of each season, being reluctant to stone the first cast.
Walter Winchell, newspaper and radio commentator, on Alexander Woollcott

....

Mr Clarke played the King all evening as though under constant fear that someone else was about to play the ace.
Eugene Field, writer, on actor Creston Clarke's performance as King Lear

....

Very well then: I say never.
George Jean Nathan, on a play called *Tonight or Never*

....

Actor: Has anybody got a nickel? I have to phone a friend.
George S. Kaufman: Here's a dime – phone all of them.

....

I don't like the play, but then I saw it under adverse conditions – the curtain was up.

George S. Kaufman

Women are like elephants to me: I like to look at them, but I wouldn't want to own one.

W. C. Fields

Miscellaneous US Insults

A psychiatrist asks a lot of expensive questions your wife asks for nothing.

Joey Adams, comedian

....

I like long walks, especially when they are taken by people who annoy me.

Fred Allen, comedian

....

She was a really bad-looking girl. Facially, she resembled Louis Armstrong's voice.

Woody Allen, comedian, actor and film director

....

Bride: A woman with a fine prospect of happiness behind her.

Ambrose Bierce, journalist and author

....

Creationists make it sound as though a 'theory' is something you dreamt up after being drunk all night.

Isaac Asimov, science fiction writer

....

Outraged member of the audience during a speech by theologian Leonard Bacon:

Why I never heard of such a thing in all my life.

Leonard Bacon:

Mr. Moderator, I cannot allow my opponent's ignorance, however vast, to prejudice my knowledge, however small.

There's nothing wrong with you that a vasectomy of the vocal cords wouldn't fix.
Lisa Alther, novelist

....

The last time I saw him he was walking down Lover's Lane holding his own hand.
Fred Allen

....

She was what we used to call a suicide blonde – dyed by her own hand.
Saul Bellow, author

....

He couldn't master mind an electric bulb into a socket.
Fanny Brice, on her husband who had been charged with a Wall Street bond theft

....

Too bad all the people who know how to run the country are busy driving cabs and cutting hair.
George Burns, comedian

....

Think of how stupid the average person is, and realize half of them are stupider than that.
George Carlin, comedian

....

He looked as inconspicuous as a tarantula on a slice of angel cake.
Raymond Chandler, author

I feel so miserable without you; it's almost like having you here.
Stephen Bishop, singer and songwriter

....

I haven't spoken to my wife in years. I didn't want to interrupt her.
Rodney Dangerfield, comedian

....

There are worse things in life than death. Have you ever spent an evening with an insurance salesman?
Woody Allen

....

I have never killed a man, but I have read many obituaries with great pleasure.
Clarence Darrow, lawyer

....

My wife has a slight impediment in her speech. Every now and then she stops to breathe.
Jimmy Durante, singer and actor

....

I am free of all prejudices. I hate every one equally.
W. C. Fields, comedian and actor

....

Accounting is a malicious extension of the banking conspiracy.
Henry Ford, founder of Ford Motor Company

....

She not only kept her lovely figure, she's added so much to it.
Bob Fosse, actor and dancer

He looked like an accountant or serial killer type. Definitely one of the service industries.

Kinky Friedman, comedian, singer-songwriter and novelist

....

A mother takes 20 years to make a man of her boy and another woman makes a fool of him in twenty minutes.

Robert Frost, poet

....

A man in love is incomplete until he has married. Then he's finished.

Zsa Zsa Gabor, actor and socialite

....

You can calculate Zsa Zsa Gabor's age by the rings on her fingers.

Bob Hope, comedian

....

Zsa Zsa Gabor has been married so many times she has rice marks on her face.

Henry 'Henny' Youngman, British-born US comedian and violinist

....

We were both in love with him. I fell out of love with him, but he didn't.

Zsa Zsa Gabor

....

She not only worships the golden calf; she barbecues it for lunch.

Oscar Levant, pianist, comedian and actor, on Zsa Zsa Gabor

Oh what a pretty dress – and so cheap!
Zsa Zsa Gabor, to another woman

....

She has discovered the secret of perpetual middle age.
Oscar Levant, on Zsa Zsa Gabor

....

The only person who left the Iron Curtain wearing it.
Oscar Levant on Zsa Zsa Gabor

....

I never hated a man enough to give his diamonds back.
Zsa Zsa Gabor

....

Just in terms of allocation of time resources, religion is not very efficient. There's a lot more I could be doing on a Sunday morning.
Bill Gates, founder of Microsoft

....

If you can't live without me, why aren't you dead already?
Cynthia Heimel, playwright and author

....

Some men are born mediocre, some men achieve mediocrity, and some men have mediocrity thrust upon them.
Joseph Heller, writer, *Catch-22*

....

A woman's mind is cleaner than a man's. She changes it more often.
Oliver Herford, British-born American writer

In silence.
George S. Kaufman, when asked by a new barber how he liked his hair cut

....

He had delusions of adequacy.

Walter Kerr, theatre critic

....

Dancing with her was like moving a piano.
Ring Lardner, sports writer and story writer

....

There's nothing wrong with you that reincarnation won't cure.
Jack E. Leonard, comedian

....

All God's children are not beautiful. Most of God's children are, in fact, barely presentable.
Fran Lebowitz, author

....

I've had them both, and I don't think much of either.
Beatrix Lehmann, actor, theatre director and author, during a wedding

....

Every time I look at you I get a fierce desire to be lonesome.
Oscar Levant

....

The Lord prefers common-looking people. That is why he makes so many of them.
16th President Abraham Lincoln

His mother should have thrown him away and kept the stork.
Mae West, actor

....

You're a mouse studying to be a rat.
Wilson Mizner, playwright

....

I'm paid to make an idiot of myself. Why do you do it for free?
Henry 'Henny' Youngman

....

An economist is an expert who will know tomorrow why the things he predicted yesterday didn't happen today.
Laurence J. Peter, educator and writer

....

The finest woman that ever walked the streets.
Mae West

....

I didn't attend the funeral, but I sent a nice letter saying I approved of it.

Mark Twain, author

....

He was born on April 2. A day late.
Henry 'Henny' Youngman

....

Gee, what a terrific party. Later on we'll get some fluid and embalm each other.
Neil Simon, playwright and screenwriter

The trouble with the rat race is that even if you win, you're still a rat.
Lily Tomlin, actor

Consultants are people who borrow your watch to tell you the time and then walk off with it.
Robert Townsend, economist

I could never learn to like her, except on a raft at sea with no other provisions in sight.
Mark Twain

Hiring someone to write your biography is like paying someone to take a bath for you.
Mae West

You take the lies out of him, and he'll shrink to the size of your hat; you take the malice out of him, and he'll disappear.
Mark Twain

Make crime pay. Become a lawyer.
Will Rogers

She was like a sinking ship firing on the rescuers.
Alexander Woollcott, writer

The more I think of you, the less I think of you.
Henry 'Henny' Youngman, British-born US comedian

Author Biography

Winifred Coles, (née Pratt) was mercilessly teased at school due to having a silly name, bad skin and wayward hair, and so had to learn to think on her feet as far as witty retorts were concerned. This negative experience led her to develop a life-long interest in put-downs and has turned her into something of an expert in the subject. After completing a degree in English Language from Warwick University she settled in Leeds, where she now lives and writes.

Picture Credits
The publisher would like to thank the following for permission to reproduce photographs.
Getty Images: 6, 29, 44, 78, 102, 118, 162 © Getty Images / 79, 174 © Time & Life Pictures/Getty Images / 8 © SSPL via Getty Images.
Corbis Images: 12 © Bettmann/CORBIS / 57 © Michael Ochs Archives/Corbis / 63 © Lebrecht Authors/Lebrecht Music & Arts/ Corbis / 143 © Hulton-Deutsch Collection/CORBIS.
Alamy Images: 96 © Old Visuals/Alamy / 182 © INTERFOTO/ Alamy.